7/11/24

Handbook of The Cleveland Museum of Art

HANDBOOK

The Cleveland Museum of Art/1969

Copyright 1970 by The Cleveland Museum of Art
University Circle, Cleveland, Ohio 44106
Library of Congress Catalogue Card Number 66-21320
SBN O-910386-08-0
Printed in United States of America
Designed by Merald E. Wrolstad

Distributed by the Press of Western Reserve University, Cleveland, Ohio 44106

Contents

Ground Floor

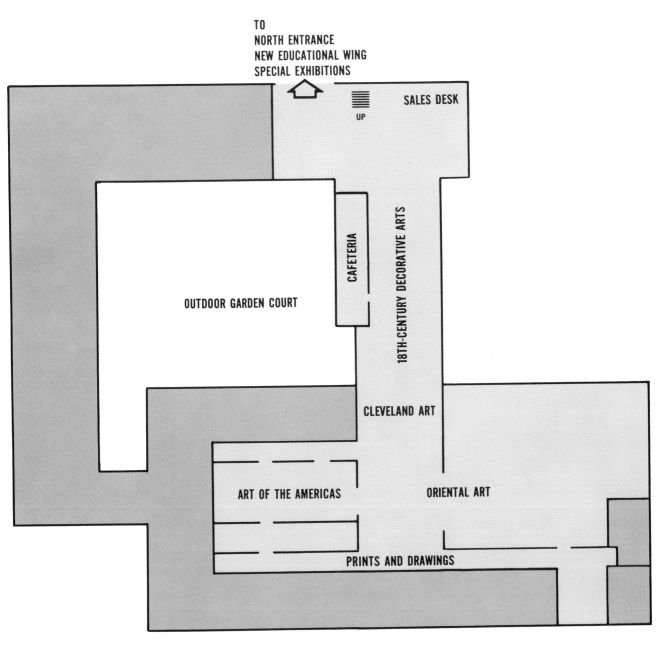

TO
NORTH ENTRANCE
NEW EDUCATIONAL WING
SPECIAL EXHIBITIONS

UP

SALES DESK

OUTDOOR GARDEN COURT

CAFETERIA

18TH-CENTURY DECORATIVE ARTS

CLEVELAND ART

ART OF THE AMERICAS

ORIENTAL ART

PRINTS AND DRAWINGS

Gallery Floor

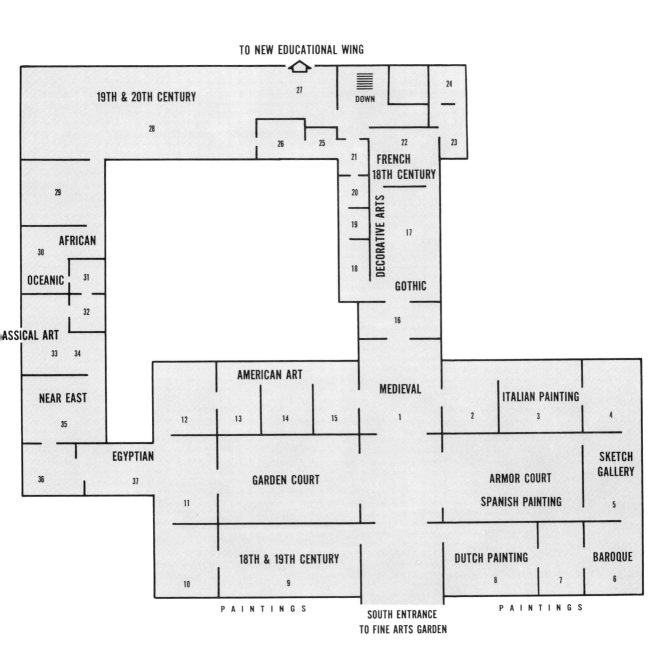

TO NEW EDUCATIONAL WING

19TH & 20TH CENTURY

27

DOWN

24

28

26   25

22   23

21

FRENCH
18TH CENTURY

29

20

19

DECORATIVE ARTS

17

AFRICAN

30

OCEANIC   31

18

GOTHIC

32

16

ASSICAL ART

33   34

AMERICAN ART

MEDIEVAL

ITALIAN PAINTING

NEAR EAST

12   13   14   15

1

2   3   4

35

SKETCH
GALLERY

EGYPTIAN

GARDEN COURT

ARMOR COURT

36   37

SPANISH PAINTING

5

11

18TH & 19TH CENTURY

DUTCH PAINTING

BAROQUE

10   9

8   7   6

P A I N T I N G S

SOUTH ENTRANCE
TO FINE ARTS GARDEN

P A I N T I N G S

General Information

MUSEUM HOURS

Admission is free

Closed Monday

Tuesday 10 a.m. to 6 p.m.

Wednesday 10 a.m. to 10 p.m.

Thursday 10 a.m. to 6 p.m.

Friday 10 a.m. to 10 p.m. during lecture season; 10 a.m. to 6 p.m. thereafter.

Saturday 9 a.m. to 5 p.m.

Sunday and Memorial Day 1 p.m. to 6 p.m.

Closed New Year's Day, July 4, Thanksgiving, and December 25.

LIBRARY

The Library is free to the public at all times. Books and current magazines are available for reference only. Arrangements may be made to borrow slides. The Library is open from 10 a.m. to 5:45 p.m. on Tuesday, Wednesday, Thursday, and Friday. On Saturday it is open from 9 a.m. to 4:45 p.m. From October through May the Reading Room is open to students holding special passes Sunday from 3 p.m. to 5:45 p.m. and Wednesday from 6 p.m. to 9:45 p.m.

SALES DESK

Catalogues, color prints, post cards, Christmas cards, *Bulletins,* books, and framed reproductions are for sale at the desk near the North entrance. A list will be mailed on request.

MEMBERSHIP

Foundation Benefactors contribute $500,000

Benefactor Fellows contribute $250,000

Endowment Benefactors contribute $100,000

Benefactors contribute $25,000

Endowment Fellows contribute $10,000

Fellows in Perpetuity contribute $5,000

Fellows for Life contribute $1,000

Living or Memorial Endowments contribute any sum above $500

Special Life Members contribute $500

Life Members contribute $250

Fellows contribute $100

Sustaining Members contribute annually $35.00

Annual Members contribute annually $15.00

Corporate memberships

Annual Members contribute annually $250

Sustaining Members contribute annually $500

Special Members contribute annually $1,000

Full particulars may be had upon request.

RESTAURANT

Tuesday through Friday luncheon is served from noon to 2:15 p.m.; on Saturday from 11:45 a.m. to 2:15 p.m.

Afternoon tea is served from 3:15 to 4:45 p.m. Tuesday through Friday; and 3:00 to 4:30 p.m. on Saturday.

Foreword

The Cleveland Museum of Art is primarily a museum devoted to the arts of all cultures, though it differentiates itself from historical, archaeological, and anthropological museums in an emphasis on the aesthetic quality of an object rather than on its purely historical or documentary value. Its origins and development present an encouraging instance of private philanthropy for the public good.

Wade Park was given to the city of Cleveland in 1882 by the first Jeptha H. Wade; an oval-shaped area facing the lagoon in the park was, however, reserved by the donor and passed on to his grandson, J.H. Wade II. In 1892 it became clear that this area had been reserved for the erection of "a building devoted to Art and establishing therein a Museum and Gallery of Art . . . for the benefit of all the people forever. . . ." The Cleveland Museum of Art was eventually erected on this land.

Funds for such an institution were bequeathed by Hinman B. Hurlbut in 1881, John Huntington in 1889, and Horace Kelley in 1890, each probably acting without the knowledge of the others. Nothing was done, until in 1913 the trustees of the two latter funds cooperated to incorporate The Cleveland Museum of Art, endowed by the Hinman B. Hurlbut Fund, with the building cost financed by The John Huntington Art and Polytechnic Trust and The Horace Kelley Art Foundation. The new museum was formally opened to the public on June 6, 1916, in the classical-style building designed by the architects Hubbell and Benes and the architectural consultant Edmund B. Wheelwright of Boston. The Museum has always been a private institution for the public benefit, and The John Huntington Art and Polytechnic Trust and The Horace Kelley Art Foundation have made annual grants from the beginning. These funds have been augmented by bequests, grants and membership support, all combining to produce a sound financial foundation for the various operations of an art museum.

Soon after the Museum's opening the first of many bequests was made: Dudley P. Allen, a founding trustee, left a purchase fund in 1915, and the

following year Mary Warden Harkness bequeathed a fund in memory of
Charles W. Harkness, as well as porcelains and paintings. Worcester R.
Warner gave money to begin a collection of Oriental art; and at the time of
the opening of the Museum the Severance collection of arms and armor, the
tapestries given in memory of Dudley P. Allen, and a short time later the
J.H. Wade II collection of paintings began a continuing tradition of giving. In
1920 J.H. Wade II established a large trust fund, whose income made it
possible for the Museum to purchase works of art for every department.

Mr. and Mrs. Ralph T. King, Mrs. Leonard C. Hanna, William G. Mather,
D.Z. Norton, Francis F. Prentiss, John L. Severance, Edward L. Whittemore,
Mrs. Edward B. Greene, Mrs. R. Henry Norweb, and others made possible
the purchase of outstanding works of art. John L. Severance and Mrs. Francis
F. Prentiss began the formation of collections destined to be among the
greatest bequests ever received by the Museum. In 1940 came the bequest of
James Parmelee, and in 1942 the bequest of Julia Morgan Marlatt established
the substantial Mr. and Mrs. William H. Marlatt Fund, the income to be used
for the purchase of paintings. That year the important John L. Severance
Fund was established for art acquisitions. It was also in 1942 that the first
of many gifts from the Hanna Fund was received, enabling the Museum to
purchase great works of art in every field. Two years later Elisabeth
Severance Prentiss left her beautiful collection, together with a substantial
unrestricted fund, to the Museum. In late 1957 the magnificent bequest of
Leonard C. Hanna, Jr., including his art collection, established large funds for
purchase and operating expenses. A complete catalogue of Mr. Hanna's
many gifts was published in 1958. The most recent example of this continuing
philanthrophy was the bequest of Martha Holden Jennings, establishing a
major fund for the purchase of works of art and for operating expenses.

It is impossible to mention here all of the other munificent gifts recorded
from time to time in the pages of the *Bulletin* of the Museum, continuously
published since 1914, two years before the opening of the Museum. The

growth of the collections, thanks to these generous gifts of numerous donors and to the purchases made possible by the various funds, made necessary the building of additional galleries, and an additional wing, designed by Messrs. Hays and Ruth, architects, was dedicated in March of 1958.

The educational activities of the Museum have matched the growth and merit of the collections. The Art History and Education Department was one of a very few pioneers in the field of children's art education, a peculiarly American development. The programs now range from those for six-year-old children to adult education, and undergraduate and graduate studies in cooperation with Case Western Reserve University. The Museum's growing publications program is another aspect of this educational activity.

Educational activities increased and diversified to such an extent that it became inevitable that new quarters and facilities were necessary to accommodate them. Several special exhibition areas, a larger and more flexible auditorium, classrooms ranging in size from lecture and recital halls capable of seating more than one hundred to seminar rooms for about fifteen students, as well as offices were all part of the concept of a new educational wing to be added to the Museum.

Because of the singular nature of the addition, the services of one of the world's leading architects was sought. Marcel Breuer and Associates have designed an extremely handsome and functional building, tying it into the original structure and the wing completed in 1950 by the simple and ingenious plan of wrapping it around the facade of the 1958 wing. Thus, the new building is integrated with the existing structures and exhibition areas, yet can also be isolated when necessary for special activities. It enables the Museum to develop its educational program more efficiently and with greater variety than ever before.

This Handbook of the collections is intended to aid the visitor before and after his visits to the Museum—before, as a broad visual introduction to the wealth of material and its particular strengths; after, as a reminder

of what has been seen, or missed. For general information on the various
areas represented in the collections, the visitor is referred to the suggested
introductory reading list which follows this Foreword. A literal arrangement
of this Handbook by galleries was not possible or desirable because of the
numerous changes and modifications required by special exhibitions, new
acquisitions, and, hopefully, improved and more meaningful sequences.
Large and good reproductions of over two hundred selected important works
(each indicated in this Handbook by an asterisk) are available in another
publication, *Selected Works: The Cleveland Museum of Art. The First
Fifty Years,* a history of the Museum by Dr. Carl Wittke, is also available.

The Handbook was the result of the concerted efforts of the various
curatorial departments. Particular mention should be made of Rémy Saisselin,
who was initially in charge of the project, and of Merald Wrolstad, Editor
of Publications, who succeeded him and brought the book to successful
completion. Thanks are due also to the Museum photographer: formerly
Richard Godfrey and now Nicholas C. Hlobeczy and John W. Cook.

Sherman E. Lee, *Director*

ART PURCHASE FUNDS

Art Purchase Endowment Funds
A. W. Ellenberger Sr.
James Albert and Mary Gardiner Ford
  Memorial
Leonard C. Hanna Jr. Bequest
Lawrence Hitchcock Memorial
Delia E. Holden
L. E. Holden
Andrew R. and Martha Holden Jennings
Mr. and Mrs. William H. Marlatt

Mary Spedding Milliken Memorial
James Parmelee
Cornelia Blakemore Warner
Edward L. Whittemore

Art Purchase Trust Funds
Dudley P. Allen
John L. Severance
Norman O. Stone and Ella A. Stone
  Memorial
J. H. Wade

Reading List

GENERAL

Gombrich, E.H.J. *The Story of Art*. London: Phaidon Press, 1950.

Janson, H.W. *History of Art*. New York: Harry N. Abrams, 1962.

Panofsky, Erwin. *Meaning in the Visual Arts*. Garden City, N. Y.: Doubleday, 1957.

Wölfflin, Heinrich. *Principles of Art History*. New York: H. Holt, 1932.

EGYPTIAN ART

Aldred, Cyril. *New Kingdom Art in Ancient Egypt*. London: A. Tiranti, 1961.

Edwards, I.E.S., *et al. A General Introductory Guide for the Egyptian Collections in the British Museum*. London: British Museum, 1964.

Gardiner, Sir Alan. *Egypt of the Pharaohs*. Oxford: Clarendon Press, 1961.

Montet, Pierre. *Everyday Life in Egypt*. London: Edward Arnold, 1958.

Posener, Georges, *et al. Dictionary of Egyptian Civilization*. New York: Tudor, 1959.

Smith, W.S. *The Art and Architecture of Ancient Egypt*. Harmondsworth: Penguin, 1958.

ANCIENT NEAR EASTERN ART

Frankfort, Henri. *The Art and Architecture of the Ancient Orient*. Harmondsworth: Penguin, 1958.

Ghirshman, Roman. *Iran*. Harmondsworth: Penguin, 1954.

Godard, André. *The Art of Iran*. New York: Frederick A. Praeger, 1965.

Lloyd, Seton. *Art of the Ancient Near East* (New York: Frederic A. Praeger, 1961.)

Mallowan, M.E.L. *Early Mesopotamia and Iran*. New York: McGraw-Hill 1965.

Parrot, André. *The Arts of Mankind*. Vol. I: *Sumer*. Vol. II: *Nineveh and Babylon*. London: Thames & Hudson, 1961.

CLASSICAL ART

Bieber, Margarete. *The Sculpture of the Hellenistic Age*. New York: Columbia University Press, 1961.

Bowra, C.M. *The Greek Experience*. Cleveland: World, 1958.

Carpenter, Rhys. *Greek Sculpture*. Chicago: University of Chicago Press, 1960.

Devambez, Pierre. *Greek Sculpture*. New York: Tudor, 1961.

Grant, Michael. *The World of Rome*. Cleveland: World, 1960.

Hanfmann, George M.A. *Roman Art*. Greenwich, Conn.: New York Graphic Society, 1964.

Richardson, Emeline H. *The Etruscans, Their Art and Civilization*. Chicago: University of Chicago Press, 1964.

Richter, G.M.A. *Kouroi*. New York: Oxford University Press, 1960.

COPTIC ART

Beckwith, John. *Coptic Sculpture 300-1300*. London: Alec Tiranti, 1963.

Edwards, I.E.S., *et al. A General Introductory Guide for the Egyptian Collections in the British Museum*. London: British Museum, 1964, pp. 222 ff.

EARLY CHRISTIAN AND BYZANTINE ART

Ainalov, D.V. *The Hellenistic Origins of Byzantine Art*. New Brunswick, N.J.: Rutgers University Press, 1961.

Beckwith, John. *The Art of Constantinople*. London: Phaidon Press, 1961.

Meer, Frederick van der, and Christine Mohrmann. *Atlas of the Early Christian World*. New York: Nelson, 1958.

Rice, David Talbot. *Byzantine Painting.*
London: Avalon Press, 1948.
Volbach, W.F. *Early Christian Art.* New
York: Harry N. Abrams, 1961.

THE WESTERN TRADITION

Medieval Art

Beckwith, John. *Early Medieval Art.* New
York: Frederick A. Praeger, 1964.
Evans, Joan. *Art in Medieval France.* New
York: Oxford University Press, 1948.
Gnudi, Cesare, and Jacques Dupont.
Gothic Painting. Geneva: Skira, 1954.
Huizinga, J. *The Waning of the Middle
Ages.* New York: Doubleday, 1954.
Meiss, Millard. *Painting in Florence and
Siena after the Black Death.* Princeton:
Princeton University Press, 1951.
Swarzenski, Hans. *Monuments of
Romanesque Art.* Chicago: University
of Chicago Press, 1954.
Wixom, William D. *Treasures from
Medieval France.* Cleveland:
The Cleveland Museum of Art, 1967.

Renaissance Art

Berenson, Bernard. *Italian Painters of the
Renaissance.* Cleveland: World, 1964.
Burckardt, Jacob. *The Italian Renaissance.*
New York: Harper & Row, 1958.
Freedberg, Sydney J. *Painting of the High
Renaissance in Rome and Florence.*
Cambridge: Harvard University Press,
1961.
Panofsky, Erwin. *Studies in Iconology.*
New York: Oxford University Press, 1939.
Pope-Hennessy, John. *Introduction to
Italian Sculpture.* London: Phaidon
Press, 1955-1962.
Wölfflin, Heinrich. *The Art of the Italian
Renaissance.* New York: Schocken
Books, 1964.

17th-century to 19th-century Art

Blunt, Anthony. *Art and Architecture in
France 1500 to 1700.* London and
Baltimore: Penguin, 1953.
Gerson, Horst, and E. H. ter Kerle. *Art
and Architecture in Belgium, 1600 to
1800.* Harmondsworth: Penguin, 1960.
Hawley, Henry H. *Neo-classicism: Style
and Motif.* Cleveland: The Cleveland
Museum of Art, 1964.
Hempel, Eberhard. *Baroque Art and
Architecture in Central Europe . . . .*
Harmondsworth: Penguin, 1965.
Honey, William Bowyer. *European Ceramic
Art from the End of the Middle Ages to
about 1815.* London: Faber & Faber,
1949-52.
Jackson, Sir Charles James. *An Illustrated
History of English Plate. . . .* London:
Country Life, 1911.
Novotny, Fritz. *Painting and Sculpture in
Europe, 1780 to 1880.* Harmondsworth:
Penguin, 1960.
Rewald, John. *The History of
Impressionism.* New York: Museum of
Modern Art, 1961.
Rewald, John. *Post Impressionism from
Van Gogh to Gauguin.* New York:
Museum of Modern Art, 1956.
Rosenberg, J. and S. Slive. *Dutch Art and
Architecture, 1600 to 1800.*
Harmondsworth: Penguin, 1966.
Stechow, Wolfgang. *Dutch Landscape
Painting of the Seventeenth Century.*
London: Phaidon Press, 1966.
Waterhouse, E. K. *Italian Baroque
Painting.* London: Phaidon Press, 1962.
Watson, F. J. B. *Wallace Collection—
London: Furniture.* London: Wallace
Collection, 1956.
Wittkower, Rudolf. *Art and Architecture in
in Italy, 1600 to 1750.* Harmondsworth:
Penguin, 1965.

20th-century Art

Arnason, H. H. *History of Modern Art.*
New York: Abrams, 1968.
Ashton, Dore. *The Unknown Shore.*
Boston: Little, Brown, 1962.
Giedion-Welcker, Carola. *Contemporary
Sculpture.* New York: Wittenborn, 1955.
Haftmann, Werner. *Painting in the
Twentieth Century.* New York:
Frederick A. Praeger, 1960.
Henning, Edward B. *Fifty Years of Modern
Art: 1916-1966.* Cleveland: The
Cleveland Museum of Art, 1966.
Hunter, Sam. *Modern American Painting
and Sculpture.* New York: Dell, 1959.
Hunter, Sam. *Modern French Painting.*
New York: Dell, 1956.
Raynal, Maurice. *Modern Painting.*
Lausanne: Skira, 1960.
Rosenblum, Robert. *Cubism and Twentieth
Century Art.* New York: Harry N. Abrams,
1961.

Painting, General

Clark, Kenneth. *Landscape Painting.*
Boston: Beacon Press, 1963.
Levey, Michael. *Concise History of
Painting.* New York: Frederick A.
Praeger, 1962.
Richardson, E. P. *A Short History of
Painting in America.* New York: Thomas
Y. Cromwell, 1963.

Prints, General

Hind, Arthur M. *A History of Engraving
and Etching.* New York: Dover, 1963.
Hind, Arthur M. *An Introduction to a
History of Woodcut.* New York: Dover,
1963.
Ivins, W. M. , Jr. *How Prints Look.*
Boston: Beacon Press, 1958.
Peterdi, Gabor. *Printmaking.* New York:
Macmillan, 1959.

Prasse, L. E. *The Art of Lithography.*
Cleveland: The Cleveland Museum of
Art, 1949.
Zigrosser, Carl. *The Book of Fine Prints.*
New York: Crown, 1948.

Drawings, General

Sachs, Paul J. *The Pocket Book of Great
Drawings.* New York: Washington
Square Press, 1951.
Watrous, James. *The Craft of Old-Master
Drawings.* Madison: University of
Wisconsin Press, 1957.

ISLAMIC ART

Dimand, M.S. *A Handbook of
Muhammadan Art.* New York:
Metropolitan Museum of Art, 1958.
Godard, André. *The Art of Iran.* New York:
Frederick A. Praeger, 1965.
Kühnel, Ernst. *Islamic Art and Architecture.*
London: G. Bell & Sons, 1966.
Rice, David Talbot. *Islamic Art.* London:
Thames & Hudson, 1965.

FAR EASTERN ART

General

Lee, Sherman E. *History of Far Eastern
Art.* New York: Harry N. Abrams, 1964.

Indian Art

Barrett, Douglas, and Basil Gray. *Painting
of India.* Lausanne: Skira, 1963.
Coomaraswamy, A. K. *A History of Indian
and Indonesian Art.* New York: E.
Weyhe, 1927.
Rowland, Benjamin. *The Art and Architecture
of India.* London and Baltimore: Penguin,
1953.

Southeast Asian Art

Frederick, Louis. *The Art of Southeast Asia.* New York: Harry N. Abrams, 1965.

Chinese Art

Cahill, James. *Chinese Painting.* Lausanne: Skira, 1960.

Sickman, Laurence, and Alexander C. Soper. *The Art and Architecture of China.* Harmondsworth: Penguin, 1956.

Sullivan, Michael. *An Introduction to Chinese Art.* London: Faber & Faber, 1961.

Willets, William. *Foundations of Chinese Art.* New York: McGraw-Hill, 1965.

Japanese Art

Akiyama, Terukazu. *Japanese Painting.* Lausanne: Skira, 1961.

Paine, Robert T., and Alexander C. Soper. *The Art and Architecture of Japan.* Harmondsworth: Penguin, 1956.

Warner, Langdon. *The Enduring Art of Japan,* Cambridge: Harvard University Press, 1952.

Yashiro, Yukio (ed.). *Art Treasures of Japan.* Tokyo: Kokusai bunka shinkokai, 1960.

PRE-COLUMBIAN ART

Bennett, Wendell C. *Ancient Arts of the Andes.* New York: Museum of Modern Art, 1954.

Covarrubias, Miguel. *Indian Art of Mexico and Central America....* New York: Alfred A. Knopf, 1957.

Kelemen, Pal. *Medieval American Art.* New York: Macmillan, 1943.

Kubler, George. *The Art and Architecture of Ancient America....* Harmondsworth: Penguin, 1962.

ART OF PRIMITIVE PEOPLES

African Art

Fagg, William. *Nigerian Images.* New York: Frederick A. Praeger, 1963.

Fagg, William. *African Tribal Images, The Katherine White Reswick Collection.* Cleveland: The Cleveland Museum of Art, 1968.

Fagg, William, and Margaret Plass. *African Sculpture.* London: Studio Vista, 1964.

Leuzinger, Elsy. *Africa.* New York: McGraw Hill, 1960.

Oceanic Art

Guiart, Jean. *The Arts of the South Pacific.* London: Thames & Hudson, 1963.

Linton, Ralph, and Paul S. Wingert. *Arts of the South Seas.* New York: Museum of Modern Art, 1946.

Egyptian Art

Ny-kau-Re. Red granite. Sakkara, ca. 2500 B.C. H. 21-1/4 in. 64.90

Tomb Relief. Limestone. Sakkara, Old Kingdom, ca. 2400 B.C. W. 68-1/2 in. 30.736

Panel from False Door of Ny-kau-Re. Limestone. Sakkara, ca. 2500 B.C. H. 46 in. 64.91

Tomb Stela of Four Persons. Limestone. First Intermediate Period, ca. 2280-2065 B.C. W. 29-1/2 in. 14.543

Amenemhet III. Black granite. Thebes, ca. 1800 B.C. H. 19-7/8 in. 60.56

3

Head of Queen Hatshepsut. Green schist. Probably Theban School, early New Kingdom, ca. 1475 B.C. H. 6-3/8 in. 17.976

Amenhotep III (wearing the Blue Crown). Granite. Ca. 1417 B.C. H. 15-1/2 in. 52.513*

Head of Amenhotep III. Rose quartzite. Ca. 1387 B.C. H. 6-5/16 in. 61.417

Three Nome Gods Bearing Offerings. Limestone temple relief. Reign of Amenhotep III, ca. 1390 B.C. W. 30-3/8 in. 61.205

Amphora. Pale green-white glass. Reign of Amenhotep III or slightly later in Dynasty XVIII, ca. 1400-1360 B.C. H. 4-5/16 in. 14.541

Akhenaten. Sandstone relief. Karnak, Amarna Period, ca. 1375 B.C. W. 11 in. 59.188

King's Scribe Amenhotep and His Wife Renut. From family tomb near Assiut. Limestone relief. Early part of reign of Ramesses II, ca. 1275 B.C. W. 48-7/16 in. 63.100

Queen Nefertiti. From the Aten chapel at Karnak. Sandstone relief. Amarna Period, ca. 1375 B.C. W. 17-1/8 in. 59.186*

Head of a Man. Bronze. New Kingdom, Theban School, Dynasty XIX, ca. 1300 B.C. H. 1-1/2 in. 14.555

The Priest Bek-en-Mut Worshiping a Statue of the Long-dead Tuthmosis III (detail from a coffin). Painting on gesso over wood. Probably from Thebes, Dynasty XXII, ca. 900 B.C. H. of coffin 82 in. 14.561

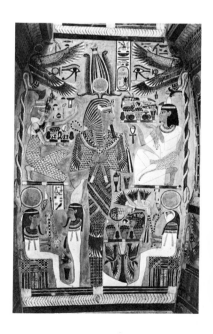

Stela of Djed-atum-iuf-ankh. Yellow crystalline quartzite. Heliopolis, Late Period, ca. 650 B.C., imitating style of Old Kingdom, H. 11 in. 20.1977

Man and Wife. Limestone relief. Thebes (Tomb of Menteumhat), Dynasty XXV, ca. 660 B.C., in the style of early Dynasty XVIII. H. 25-3/8 in. 49.493

Mongoose. Bronze. Ca. 600 B.C. or later. L. 8-1/4 in. 64.358

Boats of Mourners. Limestone relief. Thebes (Tomb of Mentuemhat), Dynasty XXV, ca. 660 B.C., in the style of late Dynasty XVIII. W. 39-5/8 in. 51.282*

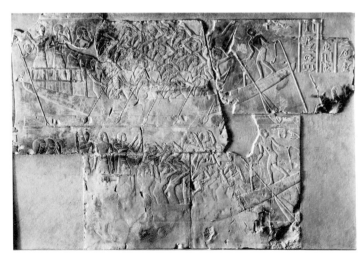

Relief from the Tomb of Mentuemhat. Limestone. Thebes, ca. 660 B.C. (details are copies from Dynasty XVIII but the servants are chiefly in contemporary style). W. 26-5/8 in. 51.284

Female Musicians. Joins to another fragment now in Berlin. Limestone relief. Lower Egyptian School, ca. 350 B.C. W. 12-11/16 in. 14.542

Horwedja Presenting a Statue to His God. Black schist. Ca. 500 B.C. H. 17-1/4 in. 20.1978

The General Amen-pe-Yom. Gray granite. Mendes, ca. 275 B.C. H. 37-1/2 in. 48.141

Notes

Notes

Ancient Near Eastern Art

10

Gudea, Patési-of Lagash. Dolerite.
Iraq (Mesopotamia), Neo-Sumerian
Period, 22nd century B.C.
H. 56-1/4 in. 63.154*

Plate. Silver, repoussé and engraved.
Phoenician, 7th century B.C.
D. 7-15/16 in. 47.491*

Winged Genie. Relief from the
palace of Ashur-Nasirapal II at
Nimrud. Gypseous alabaster. Iraq
(Mesopotamia), Assyrian Period,
9th century B.C. H. 98 in. 43.246

Crouching Woman. Ivory figure.
Syria, Phoenician, 9th-8th century
B.C. H. 1-3/8 in. 64.426

Silver Cup with Hunting Scene. Repoussé and engraved. Northwestern Iran
(Amlash?), end of 2nd millennium B.C. H. 4-3/4 in. 65.25

11

Gold Beaker. Repoussé and engraved. Northwestern Iran (said to have been found at Marlik), end of 2nd millennium B.C. H. 5-1/2 in. 65.26

Votive Pin (detail). Silver, repoussé and engraved. Iran, Luristan, ca. 1000 B.C. D. 6-1/4 in. 63.257

Cheek Plaque of Horse Bit. Bronze, cast and engraved. Iran, Luristan, ca. 1200-1000 B.C. H. 5-7/8 in. 61.33

Finial in Form of Ibex Protome. Cast bronze. Iran, Luristan, late 7th century B.C. H. 8-3/4 in. 65.554

The Bear Lady. Terra cotta. Ritual vessel from a tomb at Marlik. N.W. Iran, ca. 1000 B.C. H. 8-7/16 in. 67.35

Beaker. Silver, repoussé and engraved. Iran, Luristan, 8th-7th century B.C. H. 4 in. 63.95

Bull's Head. Cast bronze. Iran (Ancient), Urartu, 8th-7th century B.C. H. 6-1/4 in. 42.204

Ibex Head Finial. Cast bronze. Iran, Achaemenid Period, 6th-5th century B.C. H. 6-3/4 in. 61.199*

Rhyton in Form of Ram's Head. Silver, repoussé and engraved. Iran, Kaplantu, Median Period, 7th century B.C. L. 12 in. 63.479

Median Lion Strangler. Lapis lazuli. Iran, Achaemenid Period, 1st half 5th century B.C. H. 7-3/8 in. 60.175*

13

Incense Burner. Cast bronze. Iran, Parthian Period, 1st century. H. 4-1/2 in. 61.32

Lion Head Finial. Marble. Iran, Achaemenid Period, ca. 5th century B.C. H. 2-1/8 in. 62.26

Relief Plaque with Royal Hunting Scene: Ardashir II(?) Hunting Lions. Alabaster. Iran, Sasanian Period, late 4th century. D. 19-1/4 in. 63.258*

Ibex Relief. Carved stucco. Iran, Sasanian Period, 6th century. H. 12-1/8 in. 41.24

14

Rhyton: The Angel Drvaspa. Silver, repoussé, chased, and partially gilt. (Ancient) Soghdia, Hephtalite Period, 5th-6th century. H. 7-1/2 in. 64.96*

Plate: The Goddess Anahita. Silver, applied cast relief, chased, engraved, and partially gilt. Iran, Sasanian Period, early 4th century. D. 8-1/2 in. 62.295*

Plate with Royal Hunting Scene: King Hormizd Hunting Lions. Silver, applied cast relief, chased, engraved, and partially gilt. Iran, Sasanian Period, reign of Hormizd II (A.D. 302-309). D. 8-3/16 in. 62.150

Rhyton in Form of a Horse. Silver, repoussé, engraved, and gold overlay. Iran, Sasanian Period, 4th century. H. 8-1/4 in. 64.41*

Wine Vessel: Figures of the Goddess Anahita. Silver, cast, engraved, and partially gilt. Iran, Sasanian Period, early 4th century. H. 7-1/4 in. 62.294

15

Ewer. Gladiatorial Combats. Silver, repoussé. engraved, and partially gilt. Iran, Sasanian Period, late 4th-early 5th century. H. 5-1/4 in. 61.200

Plate. Silver, applied cast. (Ancient) Soghdia, 6th-7th century. D. 12-5/8 in. 67.34

Oval Fluted Bowl. Silver, cast, engraved, and partially gilt. Iran, Sasanian Period, 5th century. L. 11-3/16 in. 63.478

Bowl: The Entertainers. Silver, cast, chased and engraved, and partially gilt. Iran, Sasanian Period, late 4th-early 5th century. D. 5-1/4 in. 66.369

16

Textile. Compound twill, silk. Iran, Sasanian Period, 6th-7th century.
H. 3-1/4 in. 51.88

Textile. Tapestry weave, wool and linen. Iran, Sasanian Period, 6th-7th
century. H. 8-1/4 in. 50.509

Notes

Notes

Classical Art

20

Kouros. Island marble. Greece, ca. 560-540 B.C. H. 24-5/8 in. 53.125*

Lekythos by Douris. Pottery. Greece, 500-490 B.C. H. 12-1/2 in. 66.114

Standing Warrior. Bronze. Italy, Rimini(?), Etruscan, ca. 500-450 B.C. H. 11 in. 67.32

Red-figured Krater by the Cleveland Painter. Pottery. Greece, Attic, early 5th century B.C. H. 22-1/4 in. 30.104

Head of a Goat. Limestone. Greece, Attic, ca. 500 B.C. H. 13-3/4 in. 26.538

Red-figured Lekythos: Warrior Cutting off a Lock of Hair. Pottery. Greece, Athenian, early 5th century B.C. H. 17-1/8 in. 28.660

Athlete. Bronze. South Italy, Locri, 460-450 B.C. H. 8-7/8 in. 28.659

Athlete. Bronze. Greece, Attic, School of Polykleitos, ca. 460 B.C. H. 7-3/4 in. 55.684*

Head of a Lion. Terra cotta. Greek, from Italy, 5th century B.C. H. 4-5/8 in. 27.27

Mirror (detail). Bronze. Greece, ca. 470-460 B.C. Over-all H. 15-1/4 in. 50.7*

22

Charging Bull. Bronze. Greece, Lucania, late 5th century B.C.
L. 7-1/4 in. 30.336

Cista Handle: The Genii Sleep and Death Carrying off Fallen Memnon.
Bronze. Etruscan, 2nd half 4th century B.C. W. 6-7/8 in. 45.13*

Mirror Rest: Siren. Bronze inlaid
with silver. Greece, Corinth,
ca. 475 B.C. H. 4-1/2 in. 67.204

Grave Monument. Marble. Greece,
Attic, ca. 400-350 B.C. H. 50-1/2 in.
24.1018

Torso of a Youth. Marble. Greece, ca. 150-100 B.C. H. 40-5/8 in. 65.23

Incense Burner Supported by Dionysus. Bronze. Etruscan, 2nd century B.C. H. 24 in. 52.96

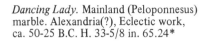

Dancing Lady. Mainland (Peloponnesus) marble. Alexandria(?), Eclectic work, ca. 50-25 B.C. H. 33-5/8 in. 65.24*

Perfume Container in Form of an Askos (Skin). Agate, with gold mounts. East Greek, Amisos (Turkey), ca. 2nd century B.C. or later(?). H. 2-9/16 in. 64.92

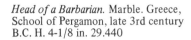

Head of a Barbarian. Marble. Greece, School of Pergamon, late 3rd century B.C. H. 4-1/8 in. 29.440

Head of a Mule. Bronze. Hellenistic, from Kertch, Russia, ca. 1st century B.C.-1st century A.D. H. 8 in. 43.68

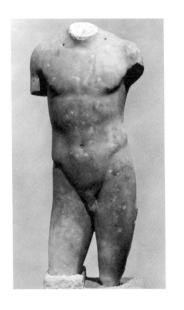

Negro Beggar. Bronze, with silver
and copper inlays. Egypt, Alexandria,
2nd-1st century B.C. H. 7-5/16 in.
63.507

Necklace. From the temple treasure
of the lion-god Mahes at Leontopolis
in the Delta. Gold, with insets of
beryl and amethyst. Egypt, ca. 1st-
2nd century A.D. D. of central
medallion 3 in. 47.506

Head of a Youth. Marble. Egypt,
Alexandria (area of), 1st century
B.C. H. 11-9/16 in. 47.188

Head of a Man. Marble. Egypt, late
1st century B.C. H. 12-7/8 in. 66.20

Vicarello Goblet. Silver. Italy,
Vicarello, Roman, late 1st century
B.C.-early 1st century A.D.
H. 4-3/8 in. 66.371

Portrait of a Man. Bronze. Roman,
40-30 B.C. H. 15 in. 28.860

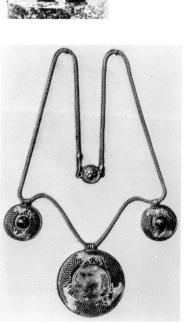

25

Apollo and Nike. Marble relief. Roman, Neo-Attic School, late 1st century B.C.-early 1st century A.D. W. 18-1/4 in. 30.522

Torso of Apollo. Marble. Roman, early 2nd century A.D.(?). H. 34-1/2 in. 24.1017

Portrait Head of a Man. Marble. Roman, ca. A.D. 100. H. 10-2/3 in. 25.944

Athlete. Marble, Roman, 1st century A.D. H. 68-1/2 in. 24.1046

The Co-Emperor Lucius Verus. Crystalline island marble. East Roman, from Alexandria, ca. A.D. 170-180. H. 15 in. 52.260*

Head of the Emperor Balbinus. Marble. Roman, ca. A.D. 238. H. 7-1/4 in. 25.945

Tomb Relief. Crystalline limestone. Syria, from Palmyra, ca. A.D. 230. W. 29 in. 64.359*

Notes

Notes

Coptic Art

30

Textile. Tapestry weave, wool and
linen. Egypt, Byzantine Period,
3rd-5th century. H. 26-3/16 in. 53.18*

Dancing Pan. Limestone. Egypt,
Coptic Period, 4th-5th century.
H. 13-3/8 in. 55.68

Textile. Tapestry weave, wool and
linen. Egypt, Byzantine Period,
5th century. H. 7-5/8 in. 16.1980

Lunette. Limestone. Egypt, Coptic Period, 5th century, W. 24 in. 55.63

Textile. Tapestry weave, wool. Egypt, Byzantine Period, 5th-6th century. H. 2-7/8 in. 41.293

Textile. Tapestry weave, wool and linen. Egypt, Antinoe, 5th-6th century. Over-all: H. 29-15/16 in. Detail: H. 14-3/8 in. 60.273

Textile. Tapestry weave, wool. Egypt, Antinoe, 6th century. Over-all: W. 62-3/4 in. Detail: H. 10-1/2 in. 61.201

Textile. Tapestry weave, wool. Egypt, Antinoe, 6th century. H. 17 in. 48.27

Textile. Tapestry weave, wool and linen. Egypt, Byzantine Period, 6th century. Over-all: W. 8-3/4 in. Detail: H. 3-1/4 in. 60.275

Embroidery: St. George. Silk on linen. Egypt, 7th century. H. 3-15/16 in. 48.115

Textile. Compound twill, silk. Egypt, Akhmim, 6th-8th century. H. 9-1/4 in. 47.192

Notes

Notes

Early Christian and Byzantine Art

Spoon. Gilt silver and niello.
Early Christian, 4th century.
L. 4-15/16 in. 64.39

Bowl. Silver and niello. Byzantium,
4th century. D. 7-1/4 in. 56.30

Bust of an Empress. Bronze.
Byzantium, Theodosian Period,
late 4th century. H. 4 in. 67.28

*The Good Shepherd and Jonah Under the Gourd Vine: Two of a Group
of Sculptures.* Marble. Early Christian, East Mediterranean, late
3rd century. H. 19-3/4 and 12-5/8 in. 65.241, 65.239*

37

Lampstand. Silver. Byzantium,
4th century. H. 19-1/4 in. 54.597

Pyxis. Ivory. Byzantium,
6th century. H. 3-5/16 in. 51.114*

Vase. Silver. Byzantium, 4th-6th
century. H. 15-5/8 in. 57.497*

Altar Frontal. From S. Carlino, Ravenna. Marble. Byzantium, Ravenna,
early 6th century. H. 39-1/4 in. 48.25

Icon of the Virgin. Tapestry, wool.
Egypt, Byzantine Period, 6th century.
H. 70-3/8 in. 67.144

*Chalice Dedicated to St.
Sergius.* Silver. Byzantium,
Syria, 6th-7th century.
H. 6-7/8 in. 50.378

Pendant with Portrait Intaglio.
Garnet, gold filigree. Byzantium,
6th century. H. 1-5/16 in. 47.33

*Paten Dedicated to St.
Sergius.* Silver. Possibly
from Benmisonas, Syria,
Byzantium, Syria, 6th century.
D. 12-11/16 in. 50.381

*Chain with Pendant and Two
Crosses.* Gold with enamel and
glass. Byzantium, probably Syria,
early 6th century. L. of chain
12-3/8 in. 47.35

*Textile: Scenes from the Old and New
Testament.* Resist dyed linen. Egypt,
6th century. Over-all: W. 41 in. Detail
H. 24 in. 51.400

Necklace with Pendants. Gold, two
garnets. Byzantium, 6th century.
L. of chain 22 in. 54.3

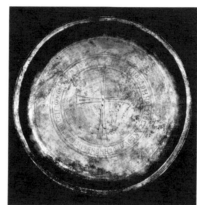

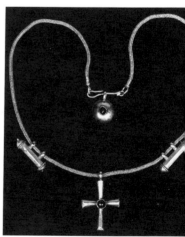

Necklace with Pendants. Gold with garnet. Byzantium, 6th century. L. of chain 18 in. 46.260

Rouge Pot. Glass, sapphire, gold filigree. Byzantium, 6th century. H. 1-7/16 in. 46.427

Monogram of Christ (Chrismon). Gold with garnets. Byzantium, Syria, 6th-7th century. H. 5-7/8 in. 65.551

Medallion: Bust of Christ. Steatite. Byzantium, late 9th century. D. 1-5/8 in. 47.37

40

St. George of Cappadocia.
Quartz (variety of bloodstone).
Byzantium, 10th century.
H. 1-3/16 in. 59.41

Page from a Gospel Book:
St. Matthew. Tempera and gold leaf
on vellum. Byzantium, Constantinople,
1057-1063. H. 11-1/4 in. 42.1512

Pendant. From the Treasury of Aachen.
1) *Relief: Madonna and Child, called*
"Madonna of St. Luke." Steatite.
Byzantium, 10th century.
2) *Frame with Winged Bull of St. Luke*
on the Back. Gilt silver and pearls.
Germany, Aachen, mid-14th century.
H. 2-11/16 in. 51.445

Single Leaf from the Epistles in a
Manuscript (Pantokrator Ms. 49):
St. Peter. Tempera and gold leaf on
vellum. Byzantium, Constantinople,
11th century. H. 6-7/8 in. 50.154

Gospels with Commentaries. Vellum;
Greek written in brown and gold,
illuminated with tempera and
gold leaf. Byzantium, 11th century.
H. 11-9/16 in. 42.152

41

Casket with Adam and Eve. Ivory. Byzantium, 11th-12th century.
L. 18-3/8 in. 24.747

*Plaque: Virgin and Child Enthroned
with Angels.* Ivory. Byzantium,
11th century. H. 10 in. 25.1293*

Scenes from a Passion Cycle of Christ. Steatite relief. Byzantium,
11th-12th century. H. 4-5/8 in. 62.27

Notes

The Western Tradition

Medallion: Bust of Christ.
From the Guelph Treasure.
Cloisonné enamel on copper.
Frankish, 2nd half 8th century.
D. 1-15/16 in. 30.504*

Group of Ornaments. Bronze and
enamel. Gallo-Roman, 2nd-3rd
century. H. from 1-1/2 to 2-3/8 in.
30.230-30.234

Crossbow Fibula. Bronze. Gallo-Roman,
late 4th-5th century. L. 4 in. 30.227

Well Curb. Stone. Italy, Venice,
8th-9th century. H. 26-1/4 in.
16.1982

Christ Blessing and Busts of Apostles.
Ivory. Germany, Ottonian, ca. 970.
H. 7-3/16 in. 67.65

Double Leaf from a Roman Gradual.
Gold and silver on purple vellum.
Carolingian, 9th century.
H. 11-1/4 in. 33.446

Reliquary in the Form of a Book.
From the Guelph Treasure. Ivory
framed in gilt silver. Ivory: Valley of
the Meuse, Liége, ca. 1000. Frame:
Germany, Brunswick, 2nd half 14th
century. H. 12-1/2 in. 30.741*

*Leaf from a Gradual and
Sacramentary (Trier Codex 151).*
Tempera and gold leaf on vellum.
Austria, Salzburg, early 11th
century. H. 8-11/16 in. 33.447

*Title Page of Abbot Berno's
"Tonarius," Dedicated to
Archbishop Pilgrim of Cologne.*
Tempera and gold leaf on vellum.
Germany, School of Reichenau(?),
ca. 1020-1030. H. 8-13/32 in. 52.88

Gertrudis Portable Altar; First and Second Gertrudis Crosses.
From the Guelph Treasure. Gold, cloisonné enamel, semi-
precious stones, and porphyry. Germany, Brunswick, Lower
Saxony, ca. 1040. Altar: L. 10-1/2 in.; Crosses: H. 9-1/2 in.
31.462*, 31.55, 31.461

Casket. Boxwood. England, Anglo-Saxon, ca. 1000.
H. 3-1/2 in. 53.362

46

Capital. Stone. France, Collégiale
of St. Melaine at Preuilly-sur-
Claise, mid-12th century.
H. 26-3/4 in. 30.18

Capital: Daniel in the Lions' Den.
Limestone. France, Saint-Aignan-sur-
Cher, mid-12th century. H. 29 in.
62.247

Engaged Capital. Limestone. France,
Bordelais (Dordogne), 12th century.
H. 21-1/8 in. 68.34

Châsse. Champlevé enamel on copper
over wood core. France, Limoges,
late 12th or early 13th century.
H. 6-7/8 in. 54.599

Front of a Châsse: The Crucifixion and Death of Thomas Becket.
Champlevé enamel on copper. France, Limoges, end of 1st quarter
13th century. W. 11-3/16 in. 51.449

Cross. Champlevé enamel on copper. Master of the Grandmont Altar. French, Limoges, ca. 1190. H. 26-3/8 in. 23.1051*

Single Page from a Decretum, by Gratianus. Tempera on vellum. France, Burgundy, ca. 1150-1200. H. 17-1/4 in. 54.598

The Horn of St. Blasius. From the Guelph Treasure. Ivory. Sicily, 12th century. L. 19-1/4 in. 30.740

Miniature Showing St. Luke, from a Bible, in Latin. Vellum. France, Burgundy, Abbey of Cluny, ca. 1100. H. 6-3/4 in. 68.190

Capital. Stone. France, Languedoc, 12th century. H. 13-3/4 in. 16.1981

Capital: Weighing of Souls. Limestone. France, Loire Valley, early 12th century. H. 16 in. 61.407

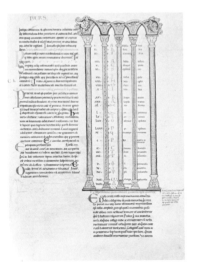

48

Engaged Capital: Caryatidal Figure Flanked by Lions. Limestone. France, Burgundian, mid-12th century. H. 13-1/2 in. 63.477

Priest and Assistants Celebrating Mass: Initial C. Tempera and gold leaf on vellum. South Italy, Benedictine School, ca. 1200 H. 9 in. 24.1010

Plaques from a Portable Altar. Ivory. Germany, Rhine Valley, 2nd half 11th century. H. of each 2 in. 22.307-22.309

Capital. Stone. South Italy, Atelier of the Cathedral of Monopoli, early 12th century. H. 14-1/2 in. 55.556

Historiated Initial A from an Antiphonary: Tree of Jesse. Tempera and gold leaf on vellum. Valley of the Meuse, ca. 1115-1125. H. 7-3/8 in. 49.202

49

Reliquary. Champlevé enamel on copper over wood core. Denmark or North Germany, 12th century. H. 3-5/8 in. 49.16

1) Paten of St. Bernward. From the Guelph Treasure. Gilt silver and niello. 12th century. Master of the Oswald Reliquary, German, Hildesheim.

Reliquary. Champlevé enamel on copper. Circle of Godefroid de Claire, Valley of the Meuse, ca. 1150. H. 7-3/4 in. 26.428

2) Monstrance. Gilt silver and rock crystal. Germany, Lower Saxony, end of 14th century. H. 13-1/2 in. 30.505*

Figure of a Prophet. Champlevé enamel and niello on copper, copper gilt. Germany, Lower Saxony, 2nd half 12th century. H. 3-1/2 in. 50.577

Portable Altar. Champlevé and cloisonné enamel on copper, over wood core. Germany, Hildesheim, 2nd half 12th century. W. 8-3/8 in. 49.431

Arm Reliquary. From the Guelph Treasure. Gilt silver and champlevé enamel. Follower of Eilbertus, German, Hildesheim, ca. 1175. H. 20 in. 30.739*

Single Leaf from a Gospel Book (now Trier Ms. 142): Nativity (recto). Tempera and gold leaf on vellum. Co-worker of Hermann von Helmarshausen, German, Saxony, 1170-1190. H. 13-9/16 in. 33.445*

Apostle from the Cloister of Notre Dame-en-Vaux. Limestone. France, Châlons-sur-Marne, ca. 1180. H. 38-1/2 in. 19.38

51

Title Page of "Moralia of Gregorius" (now Engelberg Codex 20). Tempera on vellum. Attributed to Abbot Frowin, Swiss, 1143-1178. H. 10-5/8 in. 55.74

Mourning Virgin from a Crucifixion Group. Painted wood. Austria, Southern Salzburg, Lungau, ca. 1200. H. 17-1/4 in. 57.500

Mourning Virgin. Painted wood. Spain, Castile, ca. 1275. H. 59-1/2 in. 30.622

Mourning St. John from a Crucifixion Group. Painted wood. Austria, Southern Salzburg, Lungau, ca. 1200. H. 17-1/4 in. 58.189

Mourning St. John. Painted wood. Spain, Castile, ca. 1275. H. 61 in. 30.621

Madonna and Child with Saints. Triptych, tempera on poplar. Berlinghiero the Elder, Italian, Lucca, active ca. 1200-1240. W. 20-1/4 in. 66.237

Altar Angels. Painted walnut. France, 3rd quarter 13th century. H. 29 and 31 in. 66.360, 67.27

Central Plaque from a Triptych: Virgin and Child with Two Angels. Ivory. France, Paris, end of 1st third 14th century. H. 9 in. 23.719

Enthroned Virgin and Child. Ivory. Valley of the Meuse, mid-13th century. H. 5-1/4 in. 28.760

Plaque. Gold with cloisonné and translucent enamel. France, Paris, ca. 1300. H. 1-7/8 in. 32.537

Page from the Wettinger Gradual: St. Augustine Introit for the Mass of Doctors. Tempera and gold leaf on vellum. Ca. 1330. Second Master of the Wettinger Gradual, German, Lower Rhine. H. 22-3/4 in. 49.203

Christy and St. John the Evangelist.
Painted wood. Germany, Swabia near
Bodensee (Lake Constance), early
14th century. H. 36-1/2 in. 28.753*

Lenten Cloth. Linen embroidery
(white on white). Germany, Altenberg
a. d. Lahn, 2nd half 13th century.
Over-all: W. 12 ft. 3-1/2 in.
Detail: H. 60-3/4 in. 48.352*

*Cross with Mourning Virgin and
St. John.* Copper gilt and champlevé
enamel. Germany, Lake Constance,
ca. 1330. H. 6, 19-3/4, and 5-3/4 in.
42.1091-42.1093

Angel of the Annunciation. Marble
with paint and gold leaf. France,
Champagne, mid-14th century.
H. 22-1/4 in. 54.387*

Reliquary. Chased copper gilt with
cabochons and glass inlay. Germany,
Lake Constance, ca. 1330.
H. 6-3/4 in. 32.422

Head of an Apostle. Limestone.
France, Toulouse, 2nd quarter 14th
century. H. 14 in. 60.170

54

Madonna and Child with St. Francis, St. John the Baptist, St. James the Great, and Mary Magdalen. Polyptych, tempera on poplar. Ugolino di Nerio da Siena, Italian, Siena, active ca. 1305/10-1339/49. W. 75-3/4 in. 61.40*

Madonna and Child. Tempera on poplar. Lippo Memmi(?), Italian, Siena, active 1317-1356. H. 24-13/16 in. 52.110

Two Female Saints. Tempera and gold leaf on vellum. Niccolo di ser Sozzo Tegliaci, Italian, Siena, active 1334/36-1363. H. 3-1/4 in. 24.430

Madonna and Child. On panel. Giottino, Italian, Florentine, active mid-14th century. H. 44-3/4 in. 68.206

Madonna and Child with St. Catherine and St. John the Baptist. Marble. Giovanni di Agostino, Italian, Siena, ca. 1310-1370. H. 27-1/2 in. 42.1162*

55

Cofanetto. Painted and gilded wood. Italy, Siena, 14th century. H. 9-1/2 in. 54.600

Angels. Marble. Ca. 1350. Attributed to Giovanni and Pacio da Firenze, Italian. H. 39-1/4 and 39 in. 25.1336, 25.1337

Single Leaf from an Antiphonary: Initial L with St. Lucy. Tempera and gold leaf on vellum. Master of the Dominican Effigies, Italian, Florence, ca. 1335-ca. 1345. H. 17-7/16 in. 52.281

Ascension: Initial A. Signed and dated 1308. Tempera and gold leaf on vellum. Neri da Rimini, Italian. H. 13-5/8 in. 53.365

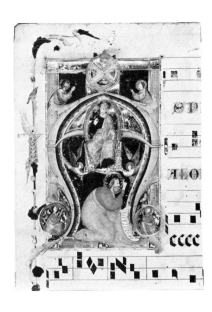

Frontispiece Miniature of the Mariegola of the Scuola di San Giovanni Evangelista. Tempera and gold leaf on vellum. Italy, Venice, 1st third 14th century. H. 10-3/4 in. 59.128

Textile. Diasper weave, silk and gold. Italy (Lucca?), ca. 1300. Over-all: H. 34-1/2 in. Detail: H. 19 in. 26.507

Albarello. Majolica. Spain, Paterna, 14th century. H. 8-1/2 in. 45.28

Single Leaf from an Antiphonary with Miniature of the Coronation of the Virgin. Tempera and gold leaf on vellum. Late 14th century. Attributed to Master of the Beffi Triptych (Abruzzi), Italian, Tuscany. H. 21-3/4 in. 53.24

Madonna of Humility with the Temptation of Eve. Tempera on poplar. Carlo da Camerino, Italian, Marchigian School, active ca. 1380-1420. H. 75-1/2 in. 16.795

The Resurrection. Embroidery, silk on linen. Italy, Florence (Geri Lapi?), 14th century. H. 16-1/2 in. 29.904

Navicella. Pen and brown ink. Parri Spinelli, Italian, ca. 1397-1453. W. 14-1/2 in. 61.38

Miniature from an Antiphonary: Historiated Initial G with Christ and the Virgin in Glory. Tempera and gold leaf on vellum. Ca. 1390-1400. Silvestro dei Gherarducci, Italian, Florence. H. 13-3/4 in. 30.105

Hours of Charles the Noble: Page 165, The Presentation, by Zebo da Firenze. Vellum, illuminated with tempera and burnished gold leaf. France, Paris, ca. 1400-1408. H. 7-5/8 in. 64.40

58

Single Miniature from a Missal:
The Crucifixion. Signed: Nicolaus F.
Tempera and gold leaf on vellum.
Niccolò da Bologna, Italian, Bologna,
active ca. 1369-1402. H. 10-1/4 in.
24.1013*

Double-faced Portable Crucifix.
Tempera on wood. Italy, Venetian
School, ca. 1370-1380. H. 26 in.
43.280

Crucifixion with the Two Thieves.
Pen and brown ink and black chalk.
Altichiero Altichieri, Italian,
ca. 1330-1395. H. 9-5/8 in. 56.43*

Girdle (detail). Gilt silver and
translucent enamel on silver.
Italy, Siena, late 14th century.
Over-all: L. 93-1/8 in. 30.742

St. Francis Before the Cross.
Tempera on poplar. Sassetta
(Stefano di Giovanni), Italian, Siena,
1392(?)-1450. H. 31-7/8 in. 62.36

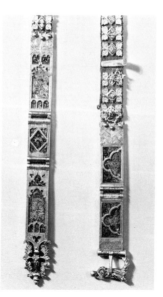

Adoration of the Magi. Tempera on poplar. Giovanni di Paolo, Italian, Siena, ca. 1399-1482. W. 17-3/4 in. 42.536

St. Catherine of Siena Invested with the Dominican Habit. From the Pizzicaiuoli Altarpiece. Tempera on poplar. Ca. 1447-1449. Giovanni di Paolo, Italian, Siena. H. 11-3/8 in. 66.2

St. Catherine of Siena and the Beggar. From the Pizzicaiuoli Altarpiece. Tempera on poplar. Ca. 1447-1449. Giovanni di Paolo, Italian, Siena. H. 11-3/8 in. 66.3*

Single Leaf from a Treatise on the Vices with Miniature of Accidia and Her Court. Brown ink, tempera, and gold leaf on vellum. Italy, Genoa or Naples(?), late 14th century. H. 7-1/2 in. 53.152

Single Miniature under Initial M: The Annunciation. Tempera and gold leaf on vellum. Ca. 1430-1440. Luchino Belbello da Pavia, North Italian. H. 7-7/8 in. 24.431*

Fragment of a Chasuble with Orphrey. Textile: Diasper weave, silk and gold; Italy (Lucca?), 14th century. Orphrey: Compound twill, silk, linen, and gold; Germany, Cologne, 14th century. Over-all: H. 42 in. Detail: H. 17-1/2 in. 28.653

Madonna and Child. Pen and brown ink on rose-tinted paper. Italy, Verona, 1440-1450. H. 4-3/16 in. 56.42

Textile (Half of a Chasuble). Velvet weave, silk. Italy, Venice, 15th century. H. 42-3/4 in. 43.66

61

Single Leaf from an Antiphonary with Historiated Initial with the Virgin as Queen of Heaven. Tempera and gold leaf on vellum. Italy, Lombardy, probably Milan, 2nd quarter 15th century. H. 22-1/8 in. 28.652.

The Coronation of the Virgin. Embroidery, silk, gold, and silver on linen. Italy, Florence, style of the School of Lorenzo Monaco, early 15th century. D. 22-3/4 in. 53.129*

Textile. Velvet weave, silk. Italy, (Venice?), 15th century. H. 15-1/8 in. 18.310

Two Kneeling Carthusian Monks. Marble. France, Paris, end of 14th century. H. 10-1/8 and 9-1/2 in. 66.112, 66.113

Madonna and Child Enthroned. Tempera on poplar. Master of 1419, Italian, Florence. H. 77-1/4 in. 54.834

62

Single Miniature of a Prophet from a Choral Book. Tempera and gold leaf on vellum. Ca. 1409-1413. Lorenzo Monaco or Matteo Torelli, Italian, Florence. H. 6-9/16 in. 49.536

Kneeling Prophet. Gilt bronze. Franco-Netherlands, ca. 1400. H. 5-1/2 in. 64.360

The Calvary with a Carthusian Monk. Tempera on oak. 1390-1395. Jean de Beaumetz, French. H. 22-1/4 in. 64.454*

Orphrey: Tree of Jesse. Embroidery *(opus Anglicanum):* silk, gold, and silver threads on linen. England, 3rd quarter 14th century. Over-all: H. 39 in. Detail: H. 15 in. 49.503

Hours of Charles the Noble: Page 395, Descent from the Cross. By the Egerton Master, with inhabited acanthus border by Zebo da Firenze. Vellum, illuminated with tempera and burnished gold leaf. France, Paris, ca. 1400-1408. H. 7-5/8 in. 64.40

Figured Medallion. From a group of appliqués. Gold, enamel, pearls. France, Paris(?), ca. 1400. D. 1-3/4 in. 47.507

63

Missal, For Paris Use (The Gotha Missal): fols. 63v-64r, The Crucifixion and Christ in Majesty. Vellum; Latin written in two columns in red, blue, and brown, illuminated with tempera and gold leaf. Ca. 1375. Jean Bondol and His Atelier, French, Paris. H. 10-11/16 in. 62.287*

Annunciation. Tempera on walnut(?). France, ca. 1390. H. 12-1/8 in. 54.393*

A Saint Bishop with Donor. Tempera on wood. Spain(?), ca. 1420. H. 67-1/2 in. 27.197

Table Fountain. Gilt silver and translucent enamel. France, late 14th century. H. 12-1/4 in. 24.859*

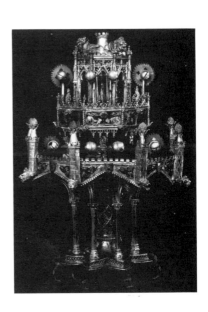

Three Mourners from the Tomb of Philip the Bold.
Vizelle alabaster (Grenoble stone). Early 15th century.
Claus Sluter and Claus de Werve, Franco-Netherlandish.
H. 16-3/8, 16-1/2, and 16-1/4 in. 40.128, 58.66, 58.67*

Leopard d'Or, Edward III. Gold.
Anglo-Gallic issue as King of
Aquitaine, third issue with English
and French titles, 1360. D. 1-5/16 in.
64.373

Mouton d'Or, Jean le Bon. Gold.
France, 1350-1364. D. 1-3/16 in.
64.372

Madonna and Child. Painted limestone.
France, Central Loire Valley,
ca. 1385-1390. H. 53 in. 62.28*

Triptych: Madonna and Child with Scenes of the Annunciation, Visitation, Adoration, Presentation. Ivory with gilding. France, late 14th century. H. 10-3/16 in. 51.450

Madonna and Child from Mariapfarr in Lungau. Cast stone. Austria, Diocese of Salzburg, ca. 1395. H. 40-1/8 in. 65.236*

The Coronation of the Virgin. Tempera on wood. The Rubielos Master. Spanish, Valencia, active ca. 1400. H. 56-15/16 in. 47.208

Half of a Chasuble. Textile: velvet weave, silk. Italy, 15th century. Orphreys: embroidery, silk and gold on linen. Austria (Bohemia), 15th century. H. 47 in. 50.85

Madonna and Child. Painted lindenwood. Upper Austria, Diocese of Passau, ca. 1370-1380. H. 20-1/4 in. 62.207

Triptych (House Altar). Tempera on oak. Ca. 1425. Austrian Master. W. 30-3/8 in. 41.68

Diptych: Four Scenes from the Passion. Tempera and oil on linen over oak(?). Austria, ca. 1400. W. 27 in. 45.115

The Death of the Virgin. Tempera on fir. 1st decade 15th century. Master of Heiligenkreuz, Austrian. H. 26-3/8 in. 36.496*

Coronation of the Virgin. Tempera on wood. Ca. 1410-1420. Master of the Fröndenberg Altarpiece, German, Westphalia. H. 26-5/8 in. 29.920

St. John the Baptist. Oak panel. Before 1425. Robert Campin (Master of Flémalle), South Netherlandish, Tournai. H. 6-13/16 in. 66.238

Virgin Mary Crowned by Angels. Oil on panel. Stephen Lochner. German, d. 1451. H. 19-7/8 in. 68.20

67

The Passion of Christ. Oil on wood. Master of the Schlägl Altarpiece, German, Westphalia, active 1440-1450. W. 88-1/4 in. 51.453

Adoration of the Magi. Tempera on fir. Konrad Laib. Austrian, Salzburg, active mid-15th century. H. 39-3/8 in. 36.18

Virgin Weeping. Wood. Veit Stoss, German, 1447-ca. 1533. H. 12-3/16 in. 39.64

Leaf from a Missal: Frontispiece for the Canon of the Mass. Tempera and gold leaf on vellum. North Netherlands, Guelders-Overijssel, Cloister Agnietenberg near Zwolle, ca. 1438-1439. Miniature painted by Master of Otto von Moerdrecht. H. 13-1/8 in. 59.254

A Bridal Pair. Tempera on fir. South Germany, Swabian School, ca. 1470. H. 24-1/2 in. 32.179*

68

Four Gospels: fol. 2v, St. Matthew.
Vellum; Latin written in black,
illuminated with tempera and gold
leaf. Germany, Middle Rhine,
ca. 1480. Miniatures by the Master
of the Hausbuch. Contemporary
blind-stamped leather binding.
H. 9-1/32 in. 52.465*

Madonna and Child with Saints. Tapestry, wool, silk, and linen.
Germany, Nuremberg, 15th century. H. 38 in. 39.162

Gothic Ornament of Oak-leaf Design.
Engraving. Master W with a Key.
Netherlandish, active ca. 1470.
H. 10-15/16 in. 52.100

Adoration of the Magi. Oil on oak.
Geertgen Tot Sint Jans. North
Netherlandish, Haarlem, ca. 1480's.
H. 11-1/2 in. 51.353

The Crucifixion. Oak panel.
Netherlands(?), close to the
Master of the Sforza Triptych,
ca. 1470. H. 15-3/8 in. 31.449

Nativity. Oak panel. Gerard David, South Netherlandish, Bruges, ca. 1490. H. 33-9/16 in. 58.320*

The Annunciation. Oak panel. Aelbrecht Bouts, South Netherlandish, Louvain, ca. 1480. H. 19-3/4 in. 42.635

Hours of Ferdinand V and Isabella of Spain: fols. 72v-73r, The Crucifixion and The Deposition. Vellum; Latin written in red and dark brown, illuminated with tempera and gold leaf. Belgium, Ghent-Bruges School, ca. 1492-1504. Miniatures by Alexander Bening and Gerard Horenbout. H. 8-7/8 in. 63.256*

A Clergyman Praying. Oak panel. South Netherlands, Bruges, early 16th century. H. 14-3/16 in. 42.632

Madonna and Child. Oil on oak. Follower of Hans Memling, Flemish, 15th century. H. 13-1/16 in. 34.29

70

St. John the Baptist. Oak panel.
Dieric Bouts, Netherlandish,
ca. 1415-1475. H. 41-3/4 in. 51.354

St. Andrew. Oak, with traces of
paint. Netherlands, Region of
Cleves, early 16th century.
H. 27-7/8 in. 38.169

An Angel Supporting Two Escutcheons. Black chalk on pink-tinted paper.
Germany, circle of Nicolaus Gerhaert von Leyden, ca. 1470. H. 8-3/4 in. 62.205

Design for a Gothic Table Fountain.
Engraving. Master W with a Key,
Netherlandish, active ca. 1470.
H. 9-3/16 in. 37.565

*Monstrance with Relic of
St. Sebastian.* From the Guelph
Treasure. Silver gilt and crystal.
Germany, Brunswick, ca. 1475.
H. 18-1/2 in. 31.65

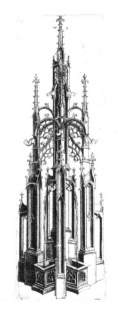

71

Abbot's Stall. Oak. France, 1500-1515. H. 10 ft., 9-3/4 in. 28.657

Madonna and Child Under a Canopy. Oak panel. South Netherlands, Bruges, ca. 1525. H. 25-1/2 in. 46.282

Double Mazer. Maple with silver-gilt mounts. Germany, ca. 1530. With portrait medallion (1528) of Albrecht Dürer by Matthes Gebel, Nuremburg and Augsburg. H. 9-3/4 in. 50.83

Chest. Painted wood. Spain, Catalan(?), late 15th century. H. 28-1/4 in. 15.535

72

The Flight into Egypt. Engraving. Martin Schongauer, German, before 1440-1491. H. 10-3/16 in. 54.260

The Story of Perseus and Andromeda. Tapestry, wool and silk. Belgium, Tournai, ca. 1480. W. 14 ft. 8 in. 27.487

The Flight into Egypt. Tapestry, wool, silk, and gold. Belgium, Tournai, ca. 1480. H. 43 in. 42.826

Plate. Inscribed: Maria. Majolica. Spain, Valencia, Hispano-Moresque, mid-15th century. D. 18-3/8 in. 44.292

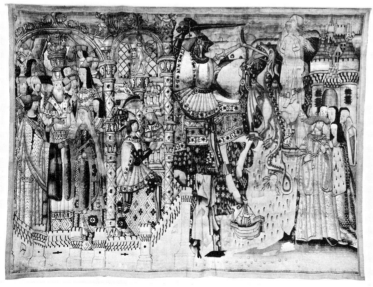

The Annunciation. Tempera on wood. Jaime Ferrer II, Spanish, active mid-15th century. H. 68 in. 53.660

Portrait of a Lady. Oak panel. Netherlands(?), ca. 1480. H. 12-9/16 in. 62.259

Holy Trinity. Poplar panel. France, ca. 1470-1480. H. 46-7/8 in. 60.79

Relief Heads of a Man and Woman. Marble. France, Circle of Michel Colombe, 2nd decade 16th century. H. 5-1/2 and 5-3/4 in. 21.1003, 21.1004

Portrait of a Nobleman. Oak panel. France, Burgundian, ca. 1490-1500. H. 16-3/4 in. 63.503

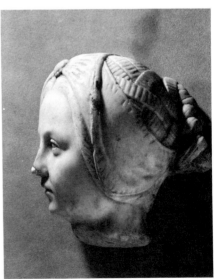

74
Mourner from the Tomb of Duke John the Fearless. Vizelle alabaster (Grenoble stone). Ca. 1462. Antoine le Moiturier, French. H. 16-1/8 in. 40.129

Single Miniature from a Boccaccio, Des Cleres et Noble Femmes (now Spencer Ms. 33, New York Public Library): *Queen Medusa Enthroned.* Tempera and gold leaf on vellum. France, close to Maître François, ca. 1470. H. 5-1/8 in. 24.1015

Education of the Virgin. Stone. France, Bourbonnais, close to Jean de Chartres, early 16th century. H. 54 in. 23.51

Triumph of Eternity. Tapestry, wool and silk. France, Valley of Loire, 1500-1510. W. 12 ft. 10-1/2 in. 60.176*

Triptych. Onyx cameo: Italy, 13th century. Gold and translucent enamel: France, late 15th century. H. 2-1/4 in. 47.508*

Youth. Tapestry, wool and silk. France, Valley of Loire, 1500-1510. W. 15 ft. 2 in. 60.177

Lady with Three Suitors.
Pen and brown ink and ink wash.
France, ca. 1500. H. 9-1/16 in. 56.40

Time. Tapestry, wool and silk. France, Valley of Loire. 1500-1510. W. 14 ft. 5 in. 60.178

Christ Carrying His Cross. Engraving. Martin Schongauer. German, before 1440-1491. W. 17-1/8 in. 41.389*

St. Lawrence and St. Stephen. Lindenwood. 1502-1510. Tilmann Riemenschneider, German. H. 37-1/4 and 36-1/2 in. 59.42, 59.43*

Pietà. Painted lindenwood. Ca. 1515. Master of Rabenden, German, Bavaria. H. 35-1/16 in. 38.294

Playing Card with King and Helmet.
Engraving. Master E.S., German,
active ca. 1450-1470. H. 3-3/4 in.
49.564

*St. John the Baptist Surrounded by
the Evangelists and Four Fathers of
the Latin Church.* Dated 1466.
Engraving, state I/II. Master E.S.,
German. D. 7-1/4 in. 50.585*

St. Jerome. Dotted print colored by
hand, state II/III. Germany,
ca. 1470-1475. H. 14 in. 52.13

St. Jerome and the Lion. Alabaster.
Ca. 1510. Tilmann Riemenschneider.
German. H. 14-7/8 in. 46.82*

Head of a Man, an Angel, and Two Small Profile Heads. Silverpoint heightened with white, on rose prepared paper. Italy, circle of Benozzo Gozzoli, 1420-1497. H. 7-5/8 in. 37.24*

Oak-leaf Jar. Majolica. Italy, Florence, 2nd quarter 15th century. H. 8 in. 43.54

Madonna and Child. Glazed terra cotta. Ca. 1460-1470. Luca della Robbia, Italian. H. 16-1/8 in. 42.782

Portrait of a Man. Oil on walnut. Colantonio del Fiore(?), Italian, active in Naples, ca. 1430/40-1460/70. H. 23-5/8 in. 16.811

The Funeral of St. Stephen. Pen and bistre ink. Fra Filippo Lippi, Italian, 1406-1469. H. 9-7/8 in. 47.70*

Madonna and Child with Angels. Tempera on poplar. Italy, Florence, School of Fra Filippo Lippi, ca. 1460-1470. H. 38-1/2 in. 16.802

Fragment: Putto Head. Marble. Close
to Desiderio da Settignano, Italian,
Florence, 1420-1464. H. 7-1/4 in.
68.211

St. Michael and St. Anthony Abbot. Tempera on poplar. 1457-1458.
Fra Filippo Lippi, Italian, Florence. H. 32 in. 64.150, 64.151*

Battle of Naked Men. Engraving, state I. Antonio Pollaiuolo,
Italian, 1431/32-1498. W. 24-1/16 in. 67.127

Head of a Boy. Marble. Italy,
Florence, ca. 1460. H. 9-9/16 in.
31.454

Book Cover. Silver and niello. Italy, Florence, ca. 1467-1469. H. 16-3/8 in. 52.109*

Madonna and Child. Tempera on poplar. Italy, Florence, School of Alesso Baldovenetti, ca. 1465. H. 38-1/8 in. 16.789

Textile. Diasper weave, silk, linen, and gold. Italy (Lucca?), 15th century. Over-all: W. 18-1/4 in. Detail: H.9 in. 31.61

Madonna and Child. Silverpoint on rose prepared paper. Lorenzo di Credi, Italian, 1459/60-1537. H. 5-11/16 in. 63.472

Life of the Virgin and of Christ: The Agony in the Garden. Engraving, state I/III. Italy, Florence, ca. 1470-1490. H. 8-3/4 in. 49.540

Madonna and Child. Terra cotta. Ca. 1478. Antonio Rossellino, Italian. H. 48 in. 42.780

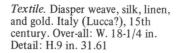

Page from a Prayer Book.
Tempera and gold leaf on vellum.
Attavante degli Attavanti, Italian,
Florence, 1452-1517. H. 6 in. 53.280

Christ Child. Marble.
Baccio da Montelupo, Italian,
ca. 1469-1533. H. 17-1/4 in. 42.799

Bust of Christ. Painted terra cotta.
Italy, Florence, late 15th century.
H. 22 in. 21.956

The Last Supper. Engraving. Lucantonio degli Uberti,
Italian, 1495-1520. W. 42 in. 40.473-a

82

St. Jerome in Penitence. Engraving. Italy, Florence, ca. 1480-1500.
W. 8-1/2 in. 49.33

St. John. Terra cotta. Master of
the Statuettes of St. John. Italian,
late 15th century. H. 28-3/8 in.
42.781

*Single Leaf: Adoration of the
Shepherds.* Tempera and gold leaf
on vellum. Italy, Siena, style
nearest to Guidoccio Cozzarelli or
Matteo Giovanni, ca. 1470.
H. 22-1/2 in. 52.282

Paneling from a Sacristy Bench. Walnut, inlaid with holly and ebony.
Italy, Florence, late 15th century. L. 68-1/4 in. 15.526

The Crucifixion. Tempera on poplar. Matteo di Giovanni di Bartolo. Italian, Siena, 1430(?)-1495. H. 13-9/16 in. 40.535

Leaf from a Gradual with Initial M. Tempera and gold leaf on vellum. Attributed to Cosimo Tura. Italian, Ferrarese School, 1432-1495. H. 30-1/4 in. 27.425

Single Miniature: Christ on the Mount of Olives. Tempera on vellum. 1490-1500. Attributed to Timoteo Viti, Italian, Umbria. H. 10-5/8 in. 27.161

The Lamentation. Tapestry, wool, silk, gold, and silver. Italy, Ferrara, after design by Cosimo Tura, ca. 1475. W. 77-1/2 in. 50.145

St. Sebastian. Brush and brown ink over silverpoint on pink prepared paper. Pietro Perugino, Italian, 1445/50-1523. H. 10-1/16 in. 58.411*

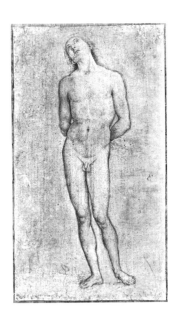

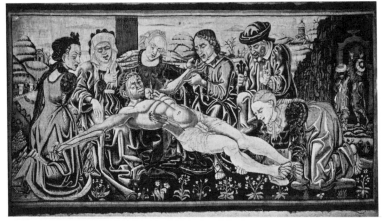

Drug Bottle. Majolica. Italy,
Faenza, ca. 1480. H. 15-1/4 in.
43.52

*Madonna and Child with St. Anthony
Abbot, St. Sebastian, St. Mark, and
St. Severino.* Tempera on poplar.
Lorenzo d'Alessandro da San Severino,
Italian, active 1468-1503.
H. 56-1/2 in. 16.800

Holy Family with a Shepherd.
Oil on canvas. Dosso Dossi. Italian,
Ferrara, 1479(?)-1542. H. 15-1/8 in.
49.185

Choral Book: Angel. Tempera and gold
leaf on vellum. Antonio Liberale da
Verona, Italian, 1445-ca. 1526.
Detail: H. 7-1/4 in. 30.661

Adoration of the Christ Child.
Marble with some gilding. Italy,
Lombardy, late 15th century.
H. 24 in. 28.863

85

Jar with Portrait. Majolica. Italy, Caffaggiolo, ca. 1475-1480. H. 12 in. 41.550

The Adoration of the Magi, the Virgin in the Grotto. Engraving, Italy, Mantegna School, after 1463. H. 15-1/4 in. 54.66

Single Miniature: The Nativity. Tempera and gold on vellum. Girolamo dai Libri, Italian, Verona, 1474-1555. H. 6-7/16 in. 53.281

Virgin and Child. Marble. Bartolommeo Bellano, Italian, Padua, 1435-1496/97. H. 21-1/2 in. 20.273

Plate. Majolica. Italy, Faenza, late 15th century. D. 14 in. 23.915

Mother and Child with Two Dogs. Engraving. Italy, late 15th century. W. 5-7/8 in. 37.566

Adoration of the Magi. Bronze. Ca. 1500. Andrea Briosco (called Riccio),
Italian, Padua. H. 9-1/4 in. 54.601

Farm on the Slope of a Hill. Pen and brown ink. Fra Bartolommeo.
Italian, 1472-1517. W. 11-9/16 in. 57.498*

Pietà. Tempera on vellum.
Attributed to Andrea Mantegna.
Italian, Padua, 1431-1506.
H. 5-17/32 in. 51.394

Hercules and Antaeus. Engraving,
Italy, Mantegna School, 15th century.
H. 9-5/16 in. 64.32

St. Christopher. Pen and brown ink with blue and green washes, touches of white. Andrea Mantegna, Italian, 1431-1506. H. 11-5/16 in. 56.39*

Base for Satyr and Satyress Group. Bronze. Andrea Briosco (called Riccio), Italian, Padua, ca. 1470/75-1532. H. 12-7/8 in. 50.375

Pomona. Bronze. Andrea Briosco (called Riccio), Italian, Padua, ca. 1470/75-1532. H. 6-1/8 in. 48.486

Battle in a Wood. Engraving. Master of the Year 1515, Italian. W. 12-3/8 in. 49.34

Satyress. Bronze, 1510-1530. Andrea Briosco (called Riccio), Italian, Padua. H. 6-1/2 in. 47.29*

St. Nicholas of Bari. Tempera on poplar. Carlo Giovanni Crivelli, Italian, Venice, ca. 1430/35-ca. 1495. H. 38-5/8 in. 52.111

Portrait of a Youth. Oil on tempered pressed wood. Bartolommeo Veneto, Italian, Lombard-Venetian, active 1502-after 1530. H. 16-1/2 in. 40.539

The Virgin and Child with St. Anthony Abbot, St. Lucy(?), and Two Donors. Oil on tempered pressed wood. Cima da Conegliano. Italian, Venice, 1459/60-1517/18. W. 31-7/16 in. 42.636

Marriage Beaker. Enameled milk glass. Italy, late 15th century. H. 4 in. 55.70

Tarocchi Cards (E Series): Music. Engraving, touched with gold. Italy, Ferrara, not later than 1467. H. of print 7-1/16 in. 24.457

Pedlar Goblet. Enameled emerald
green and blue glass. Italy,
ca. 1475. H. 8-7/16 in. 53.364

Albarello. Majolica. Italy, Faenza,
early 16th century. H. 11-3/4 in.
40.12

Bust of a Woman. Engraving.
Jacopo de' Barbari, Italian, ca. 1450-
before 1516. H. 13-5/16 in. 32.38

Plate: The Prodigal Son, after Dürer.
Dated 1528. Majolica. Maestro Giorgio,
Italian, Faenza(?). D. 8-5/16 in.
50.82

Ewer. Painted enamel. Italy.
Venice, ca. 1500. H. 7-3/8 in. 23.720

90

Bird's-eye View of Venice (detail). Dated 1500. Woodcut, state I/III. Jacopo de' Barbari, Italian. W. 39-1/2 in. 49.569

Textile. Velvet weave, silk and gold. Italy, Venice, late 15th century. Detail: W. 59 in. 31.63

Plate: The Three Graces. Majolica. 1525. Maestro Giorgio (Giorgio Andreoli da Gubbio), Italian, Gubbio. D. 17-5/8 in. 45.2*

Textile. Velvet weave, silk. Italy, Venice, 15th century. H. 17-1/2 in. 40.370

Man with an Arrow. Engraving, state II/II. Benedetto Montagna, Italian, ca. 1470-after 1540. H. 8-5/16 in. 43.65

91

Venus Prudentia(?). Gilt bronze.
Tullio Lombardi, Italian, Venice,
ca. 1455-1532. H. 7-13/16 in. 48.171

The Assumption of the Virgin.
Engraving, state I/II. Italy,
Florence, ca. 1490. H. 32-9/16 in.
49.32*

Madonna and Child. From the
Ciborium of Cardinal d'Estouteville
in S. Maria Maggiore, Rome. Marble
relief. Ca. 1460. Mino del Reamè
or del Regno, Italian, Rome.
H. 36-7/8 in. 28.747*

Plate. Majolica. Italy, Deruta,
early 16th century. D. 16-1/4 in.
23.1096

*The Holy Family with St. Margaret
and St. John.* Oil and tempera on
poplar. Filippino Lippi, Italian,
Florence, ca. 1457-1504.
D. 61-1/4 in. 32.227*

Figure of Plenty. Glazed terra cotta.
1520-1530. Giovanni della Robbia
(or his atelier), Italian, Florence.
H. 43-3/8 in. 40.343

Study for the Nude Youth over the Prophet Daniel, in the Sistine Chapel Ceiling Fresco. Red chalk. Michelangelo Buonarroti, Italian, 1475-1564. H. 13-3/16 in. 40.465

Standing Figure of a Man. Bronze Italy, Florence, mid-16th century. H. 12-1/4 in. 47.509

Sacrifice of Isaac. On poplar. Ca. 1527-1529. Andrea del Sarto, Italian, Florence. H. 69 in. 37.577*

Circular Table. Walnut. Italy, Florence, late 16th century. H. 31-1/2 in. 39.183

Plate: Sacrifice. Dated 1526. Signed: M. G. da Agubio. Majolica. Maestro Giorgio, Italian, Castel Durante(?). D. 10-5/8 in. 50.156

Tazza with Putti Frieze. Enameled blue glass. Italy, Venice, ca. 1490. H. 7-3/16 in. 60.38*

Venus Reclining in a Landscape. Engraving, state I/II. Giulio Campagnola. Italian, ca. 1482-after 1515. W. 7-1/8 in. 31.205*

The Fate of the Evil Tongue. Engraving. Nicoletto Rosex (da Modena), Italian, active ca. 1490-after 1511. H. 11-11/16 in. 47.11

Running Woman (Atalanta?). Bronze. Maffeo Olivieri, Italian, Brescia, 1484-1543/44. H. 7-1/8 in. 63.92

Venus. Bronze. Ca. 1560. Danese Cattaneo, Italian, active in Venice and the Veneto, 1509-1573. H. 12-7/8 in. 50.578

Adoration of the Magi. Oil on canvas. Ca. 1560. Titian, Italian, Venice. W. 89-7/8 in. 57.150

Baptism of Christ. Oil on canvas. After 1580. Tintoretto (Jacopo Robusti), Italian, Venice. W. 99 in. 50.400*

Madonna and Child. Signed: Iacobus Sansov. Bronze. Jacopo Tatti (called Sansovino), Italian, Florence 1486-Venice 1570. H. 18-3/4 in. 51.316

St. John the Baptist. Bronze. Jacopo Tatti (called Sansovino), Italian, Florence 1486-Venice 1570. H. 19-1/2 in. 52.276

Albarello: Andromeda Saved by Perseus. Majolica. Italy, Venice, Workshop of Domenigo da Venezia, early 16th century. H. 11-3/8 in. 20.421

St. Margaret. Marble. 1520-1530. Antonello Gagini, Italian, Sicilian School. H. 55 in. 42.564

The Assumption of the Virgin. Dated 1517. Engraving, state I/II. Domenico Campagnola, Italian. H. 11-1/2 in. 54.741

Virgin and Child Enthroned. Verré eglomisé. Italy, 16th century. Frame: Silver and enamel. Germany, Augsburg, ca. 1600. H. 7-3/8 in. 43.284

Pendant: Madonna and Child with Saints. Enameled gold with pearls and emeralds. Italy, late 16th century. H. 2-7/8 in. 59.337

The Dead Christ with Joseph of Arimathea. Oil on poplar. Ca. 1525.
Giovanni Girolamo Savoldo, Italian, Brescia. W. 75-1/2 in. 52.512

Portrait of a Gentleman and His Wife. Oil on canvas. School of
Antonio Moro (Anthonis Mor Van Dashorst), North Netherlandish,
Utrecht, ca. 1517/1521-1576/77. W. 55-1/2 in. 16.793

Portrait of Vincenzo Guarignoni.
Dated 1572. Oil on canvas.
Giovanni Battista Moroni. Italian,
Brescia. H. 24-3/4 in. 62.1

Credenza. Walnut. Italy, Brescia,
mid-16th century. H. 50-1/4 in. 39.188

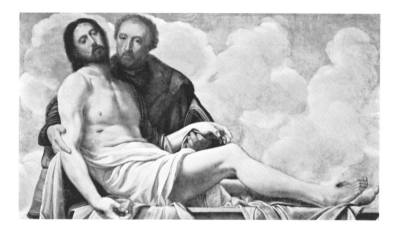

Portrait of a Nobleman.
Oil on canvas. 1525. Lorenzo Lotto,
Italian, Venice. H. 43 in. 50.250

Portrait of Agostino Barbarigo.
Oil on canvas. Ca. 1570.
Paolo Veronese, Italian, Venice.
W. 45-3/4 in. 28.16

Head of St. John the Baptist. Oil
on canvas. Lorenzo Lotto, Italian,
Venice, 1480-1556. W. 28-5/8 in.
53.424

Cassone Frontal. Walnut. Italy, 16th century. L. 68 in. 15.528

Lazarus and the Rich Man. Oil on canvas. Ca. 1550. Jacopo Bassano, Italian. W. 87 in. 39.68*

Espalier Plates. Steel. Attributed to Negroli, Italian, Milan, 16th century. H. 5-1/2 in. 16.1517, 16.1518

The Entombment. Oil on canvas. Ca. 1580. Leandro Bassano, Italian, Venice. H. 48-3/4 in. 16.806

Annunciation. Oil on canvas. Paolo Veronese, Italian, Venice, 1528-1588. H. 59 in. 50.251

Annunciation. Pen and brown ink and gray wash. Luca Cambiaso, Italian, 1527-1585. H. 11-5/8 in. 59.200

99

Apollo on Parnassus, Surrounded by Muses and Poets. Engraving, before state I/II. Marcantonio Raimondi, Italian, ca. 1480-ca. 1530. W. 18-1/2 in. 63.231

Cassone. Walnut. Italy, Venice, mid-16th century. H. 27 in. 42.607

Plaque: Feast of the Gods. Bronze. Alessandro Vittoria, Italian, Trent 1525-Venice 1608. H. 13-1/2 in. 52.464

Plate. Majolica. Italy, Urbino, Atelier of the Fontana Family, ca. 1560. D. 18 in. 42.622

Mars. Bronze. Giovanni Bologna, Italian, Douai 1529-Florence 1608. H. 15-3/8 in. 64.421*

Medici Plate. Soft paste porcelain. Italy, Florence, ca. 1580. D. 11 in. 49.489

Study for Aeneas' Flight from Troy. Pen and brown ink, black chalk, brown and light-yellow wash on gray-green paper. Federico Barocci, Italian, 1535(?)-1612. W. 16-13/16 in. 60.26*

Dressoir. Walnut. France, Burgundy, mid-16th century. H. 59 in. 42.606

The Apocalypse: St. John Sees the Four Riders. Engraving. Jean Duvet, French, 1485-after 1556. H. of page 14-3/8 in. 53.222

Chest. Oak. France, Normandy, 2nd half 16th century. H. 38 in. 42.604

Ewer with Relief Scenes of Allegorical Subjects. Gilt silver. Ca. 1580. Attributed to François Briot, French, Strasbourg. H. 9-7/8 in. 40.16

Hat Jewel: The Rape of Helen. Enamel on gold. France, mid-16th century. D. 2 in. 49.377*

Hat Jewel: Adoration of the Kings. Enamel on gold. France, ca. 1540. D. 1-7/8 in. 38.428*

Portrait of a Princess. Oil on oak.
Corneille de Lyon, French,
ca. 1520-1574(?). H. 6-1/2 in. 42.48

Mirror Back. Enamel "en resille."
France, 2nd half 16th century.
H. 3-1/2 in. 26.246

Two Allegorical Figures. Painted wood. France, Circle of Francesco
Primaticcio, ca. 1560. H. 24-1/2 and 24-1/8 in. 59.345, 59.346

St. Porchaire Ewer. Faïence. France,
16th century. H. 14 in. 53.363

103

Ewer Stand. Dated 1557. Enamel on copper. Pierre Reymond, French, Limoges. D. 19-1/8 in. 40.139

Inlaid Table. Walnut. France, Burgundian School, 2nd half 16th century. H. 34-3/4 in. 42.601

Seated Woman and Two Children (Charity?). Alabaster. Attributed to Germain Pilon, French, ca. 1535-1590. H. 11-3/4 in. 51.541

St. Porchaire Pedestal Dish. Faïence. France, 16th century. H. 5-5/8 in. 52.278

Samson and Delilah. Woodcut.
Lucas van Leyden, Dutch, 1494-1533.
H. 16-1/4 in. 35.117

Adoration of the Shepherds.
Engraving. Frans Crabbe, Flemish,
ca. 1480-1553. H. 9-5/8 in. 66.121

Return of the Prodigal Son.
Engraving. Lucas van Leyden, Dutch,
1494-1533. W. 9-5/8 in. 27.361

Landscape with Venus and Adonis. Oil on copper. Gillis van Coninxloo,
Flemish, 1544-1606/07. W. 21-1/16 in. 62.293

*Landscape with St. John the Baptist
Preaching.* Oil on oak. Herri met
de Bles, Netherlandish, 1480-1550.
W. 16-1/2 in. 67.20

Two Peasants in Half Figure. Pen
and light brown ink over black chalk.
Pieter Bruegel I, Flemish,
1525-1569. W. 7-3/8 in. 45.114

*The Apocalypse: The Riders on the
Four Horses.* Woodcut. Albrecht Dürer,
German, 1471-1528. H. 15-1/2 in.
32.313

Portrait of an Elizabethan Gallant.
Dated 1576. On vellum. Nicholas
Hilliard, English. D. 1-15/16 in.
60.39

The Dead Christ. Dated 1505. Charcoal. Albrecht Dürer, German. W. 9-1/4 in.
52.531*

Sir Anthony Mildmay. Water color on
vellum. Nicholas Hilliard, English,
1547(?)-1619. H. 9-1/4 in. 26.554*

The Arm of Eve. Dated 1507.
Brush drawing in brown and white
ink on blue paper. Albrecht Dürer,
German. H. 13-3/16 in. 65.470*

Adam and Eve. Bronze. Germany,
Nuremberg, Circle of Peter Vischer
the Younger, ca. 1520. H. 5-5/8 in.
61.29

Adam and Eve. Dated 1515. Bronze.
Ludwig Krug, German, Nuremberg.
H. 5 in. 48.359

Adam and Eve. Boxwood. Attributed to Conrad Meit, South German,
1470/80-ca. 1550. H. 8-3/4 in. 46.429, 46.491*

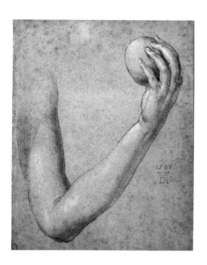

The Virgin with a Monkey.
Engraving. Albrecht Dürer, German,
1471-1528. H. 7-1/2 in. 64.29

*Plaque: Christ in the Garden of
Gethsemane.* Kelheim stone.
Attributed to Adolph Daucher,
German, Augsburg, d. ca. 1523.
H. 5-13/16 in. 47.182

Adoration of the Shepherds.
Oil on wood. 1st half 16th century.
Master of the Ansbach Kelterbild
(perhaps Hans Springinklee), German.
H. 22-7/8 in. 16.807

The Ascension. Pen and brown ink.
Albrecht Dürer, German, 1471-1528.
H. 12-1/4 in. 52.530

*The Life of the Virgin: Title Page,
The Virgin on the Crescent Moon.*
Woodcut, proof before text.
Albrecht Dürer, German, 1471-1528.
H. 9-1/2 in. 59.99

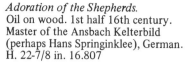

Christ on the Mount of Olives.
Dated 1515. Etching on iron.
Albrecht Dürer, German.
H. 8-11/16 in. 43.389

Medal: The Trinity. Dated 1544.
Silver. Hans Reinhart the Elder,
German. D. 4 in. 56.337

The Stag Hunt. Dated 1540. Oil on wood. Lucas Cranach the Elder with
assistance of Lucas Cranach the Younger, German. W. 67 in. 58.425

The Organ Player and His Wife.
Engraving, state I/III. Israhel van
Meckenem, German, before 1450-1503.
H. 6-9/16 in. 60.73

Sitting Dog Scratching Himself.
Bronze. Germany, Nuremberg, 2nd
quarter 16th century. H. 2-1/4 in.
60.74

109

Model for Equestrian Monument of Emperor Maximilian. Bronze.
Gregor Erhart, German, ca. 1470-1540/41. H. 6 in. 52.108

*Equestrian Portrait of the
Emperor Maximilian.* Dated 1508.
Woodcut printed from two outline
blocks on blue hand-tinted paper.
Hans Burgkmair, German. H. 12-3/4 in.
50.72*

Armet, Helmet in Maximilian Style.
Steel. Germany, early 16th century.
H. 12 in. 16.1855

The Bewitched Groom. Woodcut. 1544.
Hans Baldung (called Grien), German.
H. 13-3/8 in. 66.172

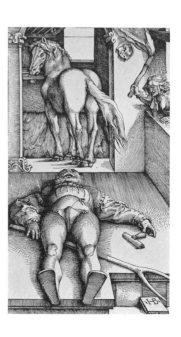

Mass of St. Gregory. Oil on wood. Hans Baldung (called Grien), German, ca. 1480-1545. W. 49-3/16 in. 52.112*

Pyramus and Thisbe. Chiaroscuro woodcut. Hans Wechtlin, German, 1480/85-after 1526. H. 10-15/16 in. 50.396

Der Weisskunig: The Banished Duke of Otnop. Woodcut. Hans Burgkmair, German, 1473-1531. H. 9-3/4 in. 60.28

Crucifix. Lindenwood. Ca. 1525-1530. Hans Leinberger, German, Bavaria. H. of figure 45-5/8 in. 38.293

Portrait Medallion. Boxwood. Attributed to Friedrich Hagenauer. South German, active 1527-1546. D. 2-7/8 in. 27.421

Portrait Plaque of Georg Knauer.
Pearwood. Peter Dell, South German,
1501-1545(?). H. 5-1/2 in. 27.427*

Pendant with Pelican. Enameled gold
with rubies. Germany, ca. 1600.
H. 2-7/8 in. 59.336

Portrait of Maria von Kitscher,
Frau Pancraz von Freyberg zu Aschau.
Dated 1545. Oil on lindenwood.
Hans Mielich, German. H. 25-1/4 in.
44.88

Model for Medal: Pope Alexander V.
Kelheim stone. Tobias Wolff, German,
Breslau, d. ca. 1570. D. 1-5/8 in.
56.28

Sir Thomas More. Oil on wood.
Hans Holbein the Younger, German,
1497/98-1543/44. D. 2-9/16 in. 57.356

Model for Medal: Son of Martin III
Geuder. Kelheim stone. Matthes Gebel,
German, Nuremberg, ca. 1500-1574.
D. 1-7/16 in. 56.25

Salome with the Head of St. John the Baptist. Pen and brush with black and white ink on brown-tinted paper. Albrecht Altdorfer, German, ca. 1480-1538. H. 7-9/16 in. 48.440*

View of a Castle. Dated 1513. Pen and bistre ink. Wolfgang Huber, Austrian. W. 8-3/8 in. 51.277

The Fall and Redemption of Man: Four Scenes from the Passion of Christ. Four woodcuts printed on one page. Albrecht Altdorfer, German, ca. 1480-1538. H. of page 8-7/8 in. 52.50-52.53

The Visitation. Oil on wood. Ca. 1520. Bavarian or Austrian Master of the Danube School (perhaps Master "I"). H. 40 in. 50.91

Standing Cup with Cover. Gilt silver. Germany, Nuremberg, 2nd half 16th century. H. 19-1/2 in. 62.286

River Landscape with Five Bare Spruce Trees in the Foreground. Dated 1549. Etching. Augustin Hirschvogel, German. W. 6-13/16 in. 51.491

Scales. Gilt bronze. Germany, Nuremberg, Jamnitzer Workshop, ca. 1565-1570. H. 14-3/4 in. 50.382*

Faïence Owl. Dated 1540. South Germany, H. 10-3/16 in. 50.370

Mortar. Bronze. Germany, Nuremberg, 1st half 16th century. Plaquettes by Peter Flötner. H. 4-7/8 in. 51.444

Sextus Tarquinius Threatening Lucrece. Bronze. Hubert Gerhard, German, ca. 1540/50-1620. H. 20-3/4 in. 62.245*

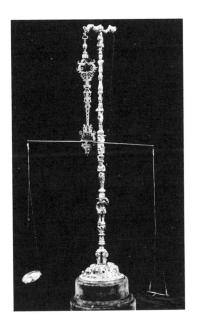

Allegory of Christian Belief.
Dated 162(2?). Pen and bistre ink
and bistre wash. Johann Liss, German,
Venetian School. H. 6 in. 53.6

Minerva. Oil on canvas.
Bernardo Strozzi, Italian, Genoese-
Venetian, 1581-1644. H. 58 in. 29.133

St. Sebastian. Bronze. 17th century.
Follower of Pietro Tacca, perhaps
Georg Petel, Italian. H. 21 in.
40.585

Pietà. Oil on canvas. Bernardo Strozzi, Italian, Genoese-Venetian,
1581-1644. W. 52-1/4 in. 53.27

*Madonna and Child with
St. Joseph and a Music-making Angel.*
Tondo. Oil on canvas. 1624.
Guercino (Francesco Barbieri),
Italian, 1591-1666. D. 27-3/4 in.
67.123

115

Study for Minerva. Black and red chalk. Bernardo Strozzi, Italian, Genoese-Venetian, 1581-1644. H. 14-5/8 in. 53.626

Pope Innocent X. Bronze. Alessandro Algardi and Assistants, Italian, Rome, 1595-1654. H. 30-3/4 in. 57.496

Venus and Cupid. Pen and bistre ink and bistre wash with red chalk indications. Giovanni Francesco Barbieri (called Guercino), Italian, 1591-1666. W. 15-1/2 in. 25.1188*

St. Jerome. Oil on canvas. Giovanni Battista Langetti, Italian, Genoese-Venetian, 1625-1676. H. 78-13/16 in. 51.334

The Feast of Terminus. Drawing in red-brown oil. Giovanni Benedetto Castiglione, Italian, 1616-1670. W. 22-1/8 in. 64.31

Baptism of Christ. Bronze. Italy, 17th century. H. 24-3/4 in. 65.471

The Blessed Alessandro Sauli.
Terra cotta. Pierre Puget, French,
active in Italy, 1620-1694.
H. 27-7/16 in. 64.36*

*St. Catherine of Siena Receiving the Crown of Thorns and a Rosary from the
Christ Child.* Oil on canvas. Ca. 1643. Giovanni Battista Salvi
(called Sassoferrato), Italian, 1609-1685. W. 33 in. 66.332.

*The Apparition of the Virgin to St.
Francis of Assisi.* Oil on canvas.
Ca. 1680-1683. Luca Giordano,
Italian, Naples. H. 94-1/2 in.
66.125

Endymion. Marble.
Agostino Cornacchini, Italian,
1685-1740. H. 25-1/2 in. 42.51

Adoration of the Shepherds.
Oil on canvas. Carlo Dolci, Italian,
1616-1681. H. 34-1/2 in. 68.22

Italian Landscape. Pen and brush and brown ink. Nicolas Poussin, French, 1594-1665. W. 8-1/16 in. 58.421

Adoration of the Shepherds. Oil on canvas. Ca. 1650. Bernardo Cavallino, Italian, 1616-1656. W. 58-1/2 in. 68.100

Samson and Delilah. Oil on canvas. Ca. 1617/1618. Gerard van Honthorst, Dutch. H. 50-7/8 in. 68.23

The Martyrdom of St. Lucy. Etching, state II/II. Jacques Bellange, French, 1594-1638. H. 18-7/16 in. 50.214

The Repentant St. Peter. Dated 1645. Oil on canvas. Georges de La Tour, French. H. 45-1/8 in. 51.454*

Roman Campagna near Tivoli. Dated 163(?). Oil on canvas. Claude Gellée (called Claude Lorrain), French, 1600-1682. W. 54 in. 46.73

Landscape with Cattle. Pen and brown ink and ink wash. Claude Gellée (called Claude Lorrain), French, 1600-1682. W. 15-1/2 in. 28.15*

Landscape with Rest on the Flight into Egypt. Oil on canvas. Claude Gellée (called Claude Lorrain), French, 1600-1682. H. 80-3/4 in. 62.151*

Charles II, King of England. Dated 1653. Oil on canvas. Philippe de Champaigne, French. H. 49-1/2 in. 59.38*

119

Dance of the Boys and Girls. Oil on canvas. Mathieu Le Nain, French, ca. 1607-1677. W. 47-1/2 in. 57.489

Diana and Her Nymphs Departing for the Chase. Oil on canvas. Ca. 1615. Peter Paul Rubens, Flemish. H. 85 in. 59.190*

Portrait of Isabella Brant. Oil on wood. Ca. 1620-1622. Peter Paul Rubens, Flemish. H. 22-1/2 in. 47.207*

Vase. Soft paste porcelain. France, Rouen, Poterat Factory(?), ca. 1680. H. 8-1/8 in. 47.63

The Feast of Herod. Pen and bistre ink with charcoal and red chalk. Ca. 1630-40. Peter Paul Rubens, Flemish. W. 18-5/8 in. 54.2*

A Genoese Lady with Her Child.
Oil on canvas. Ca. 1621-1627.
Sir Anthony van Dyck, Flemish.
H. 85-3/4 in. 54.392

Portrait of Frans Snyders. Etching,
state I/IV. Sir Anthony van Dyck,
Flemish, 1599-1641. H. 10-1/8 in.
(page). 42.741

The Lamentation. Black chalk and ink
heightened with white. Sir Anthony
van Dyck, Flemish, 1599-1641.
W. 18-5/8 in. 66.174

*The Conversion of St. Paul with
Horseman and Banner.* Ink, black
and red chalk, and water color.
Ca. 1645. Jacob Jordaens, Flemish.
H. 12-15/16 in. 54.366*

Boar Hunt. Brush with black and gray ink heightened with white. Jan Fyt,
Flemish, 1611-1661. W. 20-11/16 in. 60.157

121

Game of Backgammon. Oil on canvas. David Teniers the Younger, Flemish, 1610-1690. W. 32-1/4 in. 43.377

Peasants Drinking and Smoking. Oil on oak. David Teniers the Younger, Flemish, 1610-1690. H. 14-5/8 in. 16.1046.

Landscape with a Sleeping Shepherdess. Dated 1663. Oil on wood. Adriaen van de Velde, Dutch. W. 18-15/16 in. 66.12

Hollow Tree. Pen and ink and water color. Roeland Savery, Dutch, 1576-1639. W. 18-5/8 in. 58.315

Hilly Landscape with Hut Beside a Stream. Dated 1627. Black chalk and tan and gray wash. Esaias van de Velde, Dutch. W. 11-1/2 in. 66.7

Landscape with a Cottage and Figures. Dated 1653. Pencil and gray wash. Jan van Goyen, Dutch. W. 10-7/8 in. 29.548

The Three Trees. Etching and drypoint. 1643. Rembrandt Harmensz van Rijn, Dutch. W. 11-1/8 in. 66.334

Dune Landscape with Figures. Oil on panel. Philips Wouverman, Dutch, 1619-1668. W. 16-1/4 in. 67.124

View of Orleans on the Loire. Pen and brown ink, brown and gray wash. Lambert Doomer, Dutch, 1622/23-1700 W. 16-3/16 in. 66.4

A View of Emmerich Across the Rhine. Dated 1645. Oil on oak. Jan van Goyen, Dutch. W. 37-1/2 in. 59.351*

123

Portrait of a Lady in a Ruff.
Dated 1638. Oil on canvas.
Frans Hals, Dutch. H. 27-7/16 in.
48.137*

Portrait of a Youth. Dated 1632.
Oil on oak. Rembrandt Harmensz
van Rijn, Dutch. H. 22-3/4 in.
42.644

Portrait of a Lady. Dated 1635.
Oil on oak. Rembrandt Harmensz
van Rijn, Dutch. H. 30-1/2 in.
44.90

Christ Taken Before Caiaphas. Pen, reed pen, and brush
with bistre ink and touches of white. Ca. 1641-1642.
Rembrandt Harmensz van Rijn, Dutch. W. 9-3/16 in. 60.187

Christ Preaching (La Petite Tombe). Etching. Rembrandt
Harmensz van Rijn, Dutch, 1606-1669. W. 8-3/16 in. 58.306

Portrait of a Young Student.
Oil on canvas. Rembrandt Harmensz
van Rijn, Dutch, 1606-1669.
H. 33-1/4 in. 50.252

Old Man Praying. Dated 166(1?).
Oil on canvas. Rembrandt Harmensz
van Rijn, Dutch. H. 34-1/2 in. 67.16

*The Meeting of Christ with Martha
and Mary After the Death of Lazarus.*
Reed pen and bistre with touches of
white. Ca. 1662-1665. Rembrandt
Harmensz van Rijn. Dutch. W. 8-3/8 in.
62.116*

The Three Crosses. Dated 1653. Etching and drypoint,
state IV/V. Rembrandt Harmensz van Rijn, Dutch.
W. 17-3/8 in. 59.241

Still Life. Dated 1663. Oil on
canvas. Willem Kalf, Dutch.
H. 23-3/4 in. 62.292*

Mountainous Landscape. Pencil and ink. Nicolas Berchem, Dutch, 1620-1683. W. 20-1/2 in. 58.410

A Wooded and Hilly Landscape. Ca. 1663-1665. Oil on canvas. Jacob van Ruisdael, Dutch. W. 23-3/8 in. 63.575*

Landscape with a Windmill. Dated 1646. Oil on wood. Jacob van Ruisdael, Dutch. W. 27 in. 67.19

Esther, Ahasuerus, and Haman. Oil on canvas. Jan Steen, Dutch, 1626-1679. W. 36-9/16 in. 64.153*

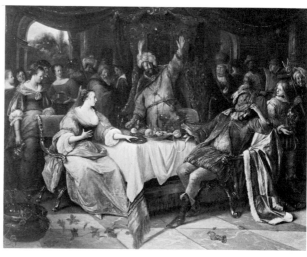

Portrait of a Standing Lady.
Oil on canvas. Gerard Terborch,
Dutch. 1617-1681. H. 24-15/16 in.
44.93

The Music Party. Oil on canvas. Pieter de Hooch,
Dutch, 1629-after 1684. W. 46-7/8 in. 51.355

View of the Heerengracht, Amsterdam. Ca. 1660-1662.
Oil on canvas. Jan Wijnants, Dutch. W. 32-1/4 in. 64.419

A Wooded Landscape with Figures. Oil on canvas.
Meindert Hobbema, Dutch, 1638-1709. W. 44 in. 42.641

Travelers in a Hilly Landscape with a River. Ca. 1650-1655. Oil on oak. Aelbert Cuyp, Dutch. W. 29-7/16 in. 42.637

Portrait of a Man. Oil on canvas. England, 17th century. H. 48-1/2 in. 46.161

Thomas Hobbes. On vellum. Ca. 1660. Samuel Cooper, English. H. 2-5/8 in. 49.548

Portrait of a Lady of the Earle Family. Oil on canvas. Sir Peter Lely, English, 1618-1680. H. 49-7/8 in. 42.247

Mirror Frame. Embroidery (stump work), silk and metal threads on satin. England, 17th century. Details: H. 4-5/8 in. 42.833

Spoon. Silver. 1661. John Hull and Robert Sanderson. American, Boston. L. 6-1/4 in. 40.214

Covered Cup. Silver and silver gilt. 1677-1678. I.A. (unidentified), English, London. H. 6-3/4 in. 58.422

Armchair. Walnut with caned back. England, ca. 1680-1685. H. 54-3/8 in. 42.573

Goblet. Engraved glass. 1680. Herman Schwinger, German, Nuremberg. H. 12-1/4 in. 50.389

Fragment of an Altar Frontal. Embroidery, petit point. England, period of Charles I, 1625-1649. Over-all: H. 57 in. Detail: H. 17 in. 19.585

Covered Cup. Silver. 1686-1687. W.I. (unidentified), English, London. H. 9-3/8 in. 35.145

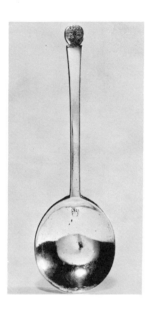

Flute. Engraved and cut glass. Germany, Thuringia, early 17th century. H. 13 in. 51.545

Covered Cup. Silver and silver gilt. 1688. Johann Andreas Thélot, German, Augsburg, H. 15-3/4 in. 66.111

Covered Goblet. Engraved glass. Bohemia, ca. 1715. H. 18-7/8 in. 50.390

Pilgrim Bottle. Polished stoneware with silver-gilt mounts. Germany, Meissen, ca. 1715. H. 6-1/4 in. 51.451

The Descent from the Cross. Dated 1653. Ivory. Adam Lenckhardt, German, active in Austria. H. 17-1/2 in. 67.134

Knife, Fork, and Spoon. Gold. Germany, Augsburg, ca. 1725. L. 7-1/2, 7-1/2, and 8-3/4 in. 63.473-63.475

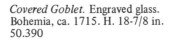

130

The Holy Family. Oil on canvas.
El Greco (Domenikos
Theotocopoulos), Spanish,
ca. 1545-1614. H. 51-7/8 in. 26.247*

Portrait of the Jester Calabazas.
Oil on canvas. Ca. 1632. Diego
Rodriguez de Silva y Velazquez.
Spanish. H. 69 in. 65.15*

Christ on the Cross with Landscape.
Oil on canvas. El Greco (Domenikos
Theotocopoulos), Spanish,
ca. 1545-1614. H. 74 in. 52.222

The Holy House of Nazareth. Oil on canvas. Francisco de Zurbarán,
Spanish, 1598-1664. W. 85-7/8 in. 60.117*

The Virgin and Child. Pen and
brown ink, ink wash, red and
black chalk. Ca. 1670.
Bartolomé Esteban Murillo,
Spanish. H. 8-7/16 in. 68.66

The Death of Adonis. Oil on canvas. 1635-1639. Jusepe de Ribera, Spanish. W. 94 in. 65.19*

The Immaculate Conception. Oil on canvas. Bartolomé Esteban Murillo, Spanish, 1617-1682. H. 86-7/8 in. 59.189.

St. Jerome. Oil on canvas. Jusepe de Ribera, Spanish, ca. 1590-1652. H. 50-3/4 in. 61.219

Laban Searching for His Stolen Household Gods in Jacob's Tent. Oil on canvas. 1665-70. Bartolomé Esteban Murillo, Spanish. W. 11 ft. 10-1/2 in. 65.469*

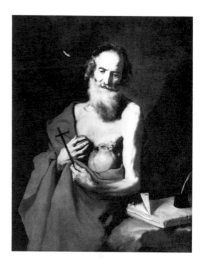

132

Ebony Cabinet. Wood, metal, and tortoise shell. Attributed to André-Charles Boulle, French, Paris, 1642-1732. H. 39-7/8 in. 49.539*

Mirror Frame. Gilded wood. France, ca. 1715. H. 96 in. 53.153

Armchair. Oak. France, ca. 1715-1725. H. 46 in. 25.1219

Portrait of Cardinal Dubois. Dated 1723. Oil on canvas. Hyacinthe Rigaud, French. H. 57-3/4 in. 67.17

Clock. Tortoise shell and brass inlay, gilt bronze. Ca. 1695. André-Charles Boulle, French. H. 44-3/4 in. 67.153

133

Study for The Romancer. Red and black chalk. Jean Antoine Watteau, French, 1684-1721. H. 13-3/4 in. 28.661

Seasons and Elements. Tapestry, silk and wool. France, Paris (Gobelin), 18th century. H. 11 ft. 9 in. 42.495

The Declaration of Love. Oil on canvas. Nicolas Lancret, French, 1690-1743. H. 32-1/2 in. 44.86

Spring. Savonnerie panel (knotted pile), silk and wool. France, Paris (Savonnerie), 18th century. H. 9 ft. 6 in. 52.14

The Swing. Oil on canvas. Nicolas Lancret, French, 1690-1743. H. 59-1/2 in. 48.180

The Minuet in a Pavilion. Oil on canvas. Jean Antoine Watteau, French, 1684-1721. H. 21-3/4 in. 38.392

134

Gaming Table. Wood and ivory marquetry. Italy, Piedmont(?), ca. 1730. H. 30-9/16 in. 53.284

Cachepot. Soft paste porcelain. France, Paris, Villeroy Factory, ca. 1735-1740. D. 7-5/8 in. 47.60

Seated Chinese with a Pot. Soft paste porcelain. France, Chantilly, ca. 1740. H. 6-3/4 in. 47.62

Cachepot. Soft paste porcelain. France, St. Cloud, ca. 1725. D. 4-1/2 in. 44.226

Portrait of Jean-Gabriel de la Porte du Theil. Oil on canvas. Ca. 1739/40. Jacques-André-Joseph-Camelot Aved, French. H. 49 in. 64.89

Cupids in Conspiracy. Oil on canvas. François Boucher, French, 1703-1770. W. 48-3/4 in. 48.182

The Flute Player. Tapestry, silk and wool. France, Beauvais, 18th century. H. 11 ft. 11 in. 42.822

Chinese Fair. Tapestry, silk and wool. France, Beauvais, 18th century. H. 10 ft. 7 in. 44.134*

The Fountain. Red, black, and white chalk. François Boucher, French, 1703-1770. H. 15 in. 52.529

The Bagpipe Player. Soft paste biscuit porcelain. 1752-1753. After a design by François Boucher, French, Paris. Executed by Blondeau, French, Vincennes-Sèvres. H. 9 in. 61.11

Mlle. de Savigny. Oil on canvas. Ca. 1748. Jean Marc Nattier, French. H. 32-1/4 in. 48.183

Bust of a Woman. Terra cotta. Jean Baptiste Lemoyne II, French, 1704-1778. H. 25 in. 52.566*

Madame de Pompadour as Diana. Dated 1752. Oil on canvas. Jean Marc Nattier, French. H. 39-9/16 in. 42.643

La Marquise d'Aiguirandes. Dated 1759. Oil on canvas. François Hubert Drouais, French. H. 39-3/4 in. 42.638

Carpet. Wool. France, Paris (Savonnerie), ca. 1750. H. 17 ft. 9 in. 50.8*

Tall Clock (Regulateur). Tortoise shell and brass marquetry and ebony veneer with gilt-bronze mounts. 1744. Jacques-Pierre Latz, French, Paris. H. 8 ft. 7 in. 49.200*

Candelabrum. Gilt bronze. Attributed to Jean Joseph de Saint-Germain, French, Paris, 1720-1791. H. 28-1/2 in. 46.81*

Commode. Wood marquetry with gilt-bronze mounts. France, Paris, ca. 1750. L. 61-5/8 in. 42.497

Gilt-bronze Clock. France, mid-18th century. H. 36-5/8 in. 51.550

Wall Clock. Gilt bronze. France, mid-18th century. H. 46 in. 50.376

Porcelain Vase. Germany, Meissen, 1749. Gilt-bronze mounts: France, Paris, mid-18th century. H. 12-1/4 in. 44.230

Pair of Fire Dogs. Gilt bronze. 1752. Jacques Caffieri, French, Paris. H. 17-3/8 in. 42.799, 42.800*

Candelabrum. Silver. 1758. François Thomas Germain, French, Paris, H. 15 in. 40.14

Pair of Parrots. Porcelain. Ca. 1740. Modeled by Johann Joachim Kaendler, German, Meissen. *Pair of Candelabra.* Gilt bronze. France, Paris, mid-18th century. H. 7-7/16 in. 38.305-38.308

139

Six Miniatures. Gouache on card.
1753. Louis Nicholas van
Blarenberghe, French.
Rectangular Box. Gold. 1753-1754.
Jean Charles Ducrollay, French,
Paris. H. 1-5/16 in. 57.412

Laban Cherchant Ses Dieux. Oil on
canvas. Ca. 1753. Gabriel de Saint-
Aubin, French. W. 21-5/8 in. 65.548

Fête in a Park with Costumed Dancers. Ink, ink and water-color washes,
over pencil indications. Ca. 1760-1765. Gabriel de Saint-Aubin, French.
W. 12-5/16 in. 66.124

Covered Bowl. Soft paste porcelain.
France, Vincennes, ca. 1745. H. 6 in.
44.225

Tureen. Soft paste porcelain.
France, Vincennes, ca. 1752.
H. 10-1/8 in. 52.3*

Tureen. Soft paste porcelain. France, Vincennes-Sèvres, probably 1756. H. 9-1/2 in. 49.15

Monkey on a Dog. Soft paste porcelain. France, Mennecy, mid-18th century. H. 6-1/4 in. 53.269

Cachepot. Faïence. France, Marseilles, Robert Factory, ca. 1765. H. 7 in. 62.379

Tureen with Platter. Soft paste porcelain. France, Sèvres, 1757. Tureen H. 9-1/2 in. Platter L. 16 in. 53.25

Covered Bowl. Faïence. France, St. Clement, ca. 1775. H. 5-1/4 in. 61.2

Morpheus. Oil on canvas. Jean Honoré Fragonard, French, 1732-1806. W. 51-1/8 in. 63.502

Young Boy Dressed in a Red-lined Cloak (the Artist's Son?). Oil on canvas. Ca. 1789. Jean Honoré Fragonard, French. H. 8-1/4 in. 42.49

Self Portrait. Oil on canvas. Lié Louis Périn, French, 1753-1817. H. 24-7/8 in. 61.334

Invocation to Love. Pen and brown ink and ink wash. Jean Honoré Fragonard, French, 1732-1806. W. 16-3/8 in. 43.657*

Table-desk (Bureau plat). Wood marquetry with gilt-bronze mounts. Bernard van Risen Burgh II, French, Paris, active ca. 1730-1765/66. H. 29-1/2 in. 44.123*

Straw Marquetry Desk. France, 3rd quarter 18th century. H. 38-1/4 in. 42.40

Table-desk. Wood marquetry with gilt-bronze mounts. Jacques Dubois, French, Paris, 1693-1763. H. 31-1/2 in. 42.591

The Synagogue. Oil on canvas. Alessandro Magnasco, Italian, Genoa, 1667-1749. W. 58-5/8 in. 30.22*

The Assumption of the Virgin.
Oil on canvas (modello). 1744.
Giovanni Battista Piazzetta,
Italian, Venice. H. 28-3/16 in.
55.165

David and Goliath. Terra cotta. 1723.
Giovanni Battista Foggini, Italian,
Florence. H. 16-1/4 in. 66.126

The Supper at Emmaus. Oil on canvas.
Giovanni Battista Piazzetta, Italian,
Venice, 1682-1754. W. 55-5/8 in.
31.245

Il fiorellin d'amore (Little Flower of Love). Black charcoal
heightened with white chalk. Giovanni Battista Piazzetta,
Italian, Venice, 1682-1754. W. 21-5/8 in. 38.387*

The Rest on the Flight into Egypt. Terra cotta. Giuseppe
Mazza, Italian, Bologna, 1653-1741. H. 12-5/8 in. 64.427

Horatius Cocles Swimming the Tiber. Oil on canvas. Giovanni Battista Tiepolo, Italian, Venice, 1696-1770. W. 82-1/4 in. 49.572

The Adoration of the Magi. Pen and brush and bistre ink. Giovanni Battista Tiepolo, Italian, 1696-1770. H. 15-1/4 in. 44.474

Horatius Cocles Defending Rome Against the Etruscans. Oil on canvas. Giovanni Battista Tiepolo, Italian, Venice, 1696-1770. W. 82 in. 49.571

The Flight into Egypt: The Holy Family Embarking in a Small Boat. Pen and bistre ink and bistre wash. Giovanni Battista Tiepolo, Italian, Venice, 1696-1770. W. 17-9/16 in. 29.443*

Martyrdom of St. Sebastian: Modello for Diessen Altarpiece. Oil on canvas. Ca. 1739. Giovanni Battista Tiepolo, Italian, Venice. H. 20-3/4 in. 46.277

Portrait of a Lady. Oil on canvas. Giovanni Battista Tiepolo, Italian, Venice, 1696-1770. H. 24-5/8 in. 52.541

The Sacrifice of Isaac. Oil on canvas. Giovanni Antonio Guardi, Italian, Venice, 1698-1760. W. 29-3/4 in. 52.235

The Angels Appearing to Abraham. Oil on canvas. Giovanni Antonio Guardi, Italian, Venice, 1698-1760. W. 29-3/4 in. 52.237

Abraham Welcoming the Three Angels. Oil on canvas. Giovanni Antonio Guardi, Italian, Venice, 1698-1760. W. 29-3/4 in. 52.238

View of the Piazza San Marco, Venice, and the Piazzetta Looking Toward San Giorgio Maggiore. Oil on canvas. Giovanni Antonio Canale (called Canaletto), Italian, Venice, 1697-1768. W. 91-1/2 in. 62.169*

Tobias and the Angel. Oil on canvas. Giovanni Antonio Guardi, Italian, Venice, 1698-1760. W. 29-3/4 in. 52.236

Views of Venice and Environs: The Tower of Malghera. Etching, state I/II. Giovanni Antonio Canale (called Canaletto), Italian, Venice, 1697-1768. W. 17-1/8 in. 25.1240

Woman and Man. Porcelain. Italy, Naples, Capo-di-Monte, mid-18th century. H. 7-1/4 in. 50.569

Standing Woman. Porcelain. Italy, Naples, Capo-di-Monte, mid-18th century. H. 8 in. 50.570

Imaginary View: A Palace on the Shore of the Lagoon. Pen and brown ink with gray wash. Giovanni Antonio Canale (called Canaletto), Italian, Venice, 1697-1768. W. 16-9/16 in. 30.23*

Pietà. Oil on canvas. Giuseppe Bazzani, Italian, 1690-1769. W. 55-3/4 in. 55.682

Visit of the Pope in Venice: The Pope Greets the Representatives of La Serenissima. Oil on canvas. 1782. Francesco Guardi, Italian, Venice. W. 27-1/4 in. 49.187

A Procession of Triumphal Cars in Piazzo S. Marco, Venice. Pen and bistre ink and bistre wash. 1782. Francesco Guardi, Italian, Venice. W. 14-7/16 in. 55.164

Visit of the Pope in Venice: Pontifical Ceremony in the Church of SS. Giovanni e Paolo. Oil on canvas. 1782. Francesco Guardi, Italian, Venice. W. 27-1/8 in. 49.188

The Spring Shower. Pen and bistre ink and bistre wash. Giovanni Domenico Tiepolo, Italian, Venice, 1727-1804. W. 16-1/4 in. 37.573*

The Prisons: An Immense Interior with a Drawbridge. Etching, state I/III. Giovanni Battista Piranesi, Italian, 1720-1778. H. 20-1/2 in. 41.30

God the Father. Painted and gilded wood. Johann Peter Schwanthaler the Elder, Austrian, 1720-1795. H. 55-3/4 in. 61.30

House Altarpiece. Carved and gilded wood. Ca. 1740. Joseph Matthias Götz, German, active Austria. H. 65 in. 64.357*

St. Joachim. Gilded wood. Joseph Anton Feuchtmeyer (or his circle), South German, 1696-1770. H. 50-3/4 in. 62.246

Christ at the Column. Dated 1756. Gilt bronze. Johann Baptist Hagenauer, Austrian. H. 7-1/2 in. 53.286*

The Presentation of Christ in the Temple. Oil on canvas. Franz Anton Maulbertsch, Austrian, 1724-1796. H. 27-3/8 in. 63.326

Kneeling Saint. Painted and gilded wood. Johann Baptist Straub, German, Munich, 1704-1784. H. 46-1/2 in. 61.414

Putto. Painted and gilded wood. Workshop of Franz Ignaz Günther, German, Bavaria, 1725-1775. H. 22-3/4 in. 61.413

Kneeling Angel. Carved wood. Ca. 1760. Franz Ignaz Günther, German, Bavaria, 1725-1775. H. 31-3/8 in. 66.18

Spring. Painted and gilded wood. Ferdinand Tietz (or Dietz), Bohemia, 1708-Germany, Franconia, 1777. H. 5-1/2 in. 62.209

Madonna of the Immaculate Conception. Painted and gilded wood. Franz Ignaz Günther, German, Bavaria, 1725-1775. H. 30-1/2 in. 63.294*

Console Table. Made for Schloss Seehof, Franconia. Gilded wood. Attributed to Ferdinand Tietz (or Dietz), Bohemia, 1708-Germany, Franconia, 1777. H. 33-3/4 in. 62.63

151

Clock. Carved and gilded wood, faïence. Ca. 1750. Works by Baumgartinger, Mergentheim, Germany. H. 38-1/2 in. 66.362

Harmony. Porcelain. Ca. 1740. Modeled by Johann Joachim Kaendler, German, Meissen. H. 6 in. 50.79

Monteith. Dated 1715-1716. Silver gilt. Benjamin Pyne, English. H. 10-5/8 in. 65.467

Pluto. Porcelain. Ca. 1760. Modeled by Franz Anton Bustelli, German, Munich, Nymphenburg Factory. H. 4 in. 47.283

Box. Gold, mother-of-pearl. Austria, Vienna(?), ca. 1765. H. 3-5/8 in. 67.157

Gilt-bronze Dish. Germany(?), 18th century. H. 12-9/16 in. 55.69

Count Tschernitscheff, Russian Ambassador at Vienna. On ivory. Friedrich Heinrich Füger. German, 1751-1818. D. 4 in. 42.1141

Tea Caddy. Silver gilt. 1741-1742. Paul de Lamerie, English, London, H. 5-1/4 in. 43.179

Punch Bowl. Soft paste porcelain. England, Worcester, ca. 1770. D. 10-7/8 in. 38.331

Teapot. Silver. Nathaniel Hurd, American, Boston, 1729-1777. H. 5-3/4 in. 40.228*

Tankard. Silver. Edward Winslow, American, Boston, 1669-1753. H. 7-1/2 in. 40.283

Brazier. Silver with wood handle and feet. John Potwine, American, Boston, 1698-1792. H. 3-1/4 in. 40.248

The Ladies Amabel and Mary Jemima Yorke. Oil on canvas. 1761. Sir Joshua Reynolds, English. H. 77 in. 42.645*

Scene with a Road Winding Through a Wood. Pen and brown ink and gray wash. Thomas Gainsborough, English, 1727-1788. W. 9-7/8 in. 29.547

Mrs. Thomas Samuel Joliffe. Oil on canvas. Gainsborough Dupont, English, 1754-1797. H. 30-1/4 in. 42.640

Young Man in Blue. Dated 1778. On ivory. John Smart, English. H. 1-7/16 in. 40.1219

A Storm Behind the Isle of Wight. Oil on canvas. Julius Ibbetson, English,
1759-1817. W. 26-5/8 in. 48.461

Portrait of Charles Apthorp.
Dated 1748. Oil on canvas. Robert
Feke, American. H. 50 in. 19.1006

Portrait of Mrs. Theodore Atkinson.
Dated 1760. Oil on canvas. Joseph
Blackburn, American. H. 49-1/8 in.
19.1005

Portrait of Mrs. Thomas Bulfinch.
Oil on canvas. Ca. 1733. John
Smibert, American. H. 29-3/4 in.
3919.20

Chest of Drawers with Panels of Oriental Lacquer. Ebony veneer, Japanese lacquer panels, gilt-bronze mounts. René Dubois, French, Paris, 1737-1799. H. 34-3/16 in. 44.113*

Roman Ruins, Villa Pamfili. Dated 1774. Pen and brown ink; blue, gray, and red-brown water color. Hubert Robert, French. W. 17-1/2 in. 51.485

Armchair (one of a pair). Carved and gilded wood. Jacques-Jean-Baptiste Tilliard (called Jean Baptiste II Tilliard), French, Paris, active 1752-1797. H. 40-3/8 in. 27.424

Young Girl. Terra cotta. Claude Michel (called Clodion), French, 1738-1814. H. 17-3/4 in. 42.50*

Satyress and Child. Terra cotta. 1803. Claude Michel (called Clodion), French. D. 12-1/8 in. 63.251

Fire Dog (one of a pair). Gilt bronze. France, ca. 1785. H. 18-1/4 in. 44.126

Candelabrum. Bronze and gilt bronze with marble base. Claude Michel (called Clodion), French, 1738-1814. H. 63-1/8 in. 44.125

Textile Panel. Silk, *lampas* weave, brocaded and embroidered. France, Lyon (design by Jean Démosthène Dugourc), ca. 1790. H. 93-1/4 in. 35.237

Candelabrum. Bronze, gilt bronze and gray marble. Claude Michel (called Clodion), French, 1738-1814. H. 36-1/4 in. 42.59

Work Table. Wood marquetry with gilt-bronze mounts, Sèvres porcelain top. Martin Carlin, French, Paris, active 1766-1785. H. 30-1/2 in. 42.594

Small Writing Table. Wood marquetry with gilt-bronze mounts. Jean-François Leleu, French, Paris, 1729-1807. H. 29 in. 44.115

Armchair (one of a pair). Carved and partially gilded wood. Nicholas-Denis Delaisement, French, Paris, active 1776-after 1792. H. 38-5/8 in. 44.110

Table. Mahogany with gilt-bronze mounts and white marble top. Adam Weisweiler, French, Paris, ca. 1750-ca. 1809. H. 36 in. 22.73

Stool. Made for Marie Antoinette's game room at Compiègne, but used at Fontainebleau. Carved and gilded wood. 1786-1787. Jean-Baptiste-Claude Sené, French, Paris H. 17-5/8 in. 54.385

Chair (one of a set of four). Carved, painted, and gilded wood with Beauvais tapestry covers. Georges Jacob, French, Paris, 1739-1814. H. 35-5/8 in. 42.75

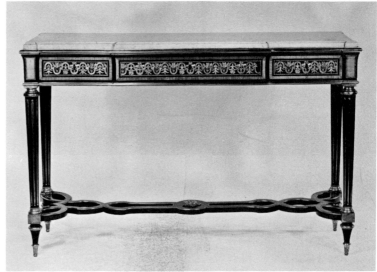

159

Tureen and Platter. Silver. 1798-1809. Henri Auguste, French, Paris.
Tureen H. 10-5/16 in. Platter D. 19-3/8 in. 52.592

Armchair (one of a set of six chairs and a settee). Carved and painted wood, covered in Aubusson tapestry after a design by Huet. Henri Jacob, French, Paris, 1753-1824. H. 38 in. 42.30

Six Miniatures Mounted in an Oval Box. Dated 1779-1780(?). Gouache miniatures mounted in gold and enamel. Painted by Pierre Marie Gault de Saint-Germain, French, Paris. H. 1-5/16 in. 57.409*

Rectangular Box. Enamel on gold. France, Paris, 1768-1769(?). H. 1-3/4 in. 57.410

Lady Louisa Manners, Later Countess of Dysart, as Juno. Oil on canvas. Sir Thomas Lawrence, English, 1769-1830. H. 100-1/2 in. 61.220

The Daughters of Colonel Thomas Carteret Hardy. Oil on canvas. 1801. Sir Thomas Lawrence, English. H. 50-3/4 in. 42.642

Portrait of Mrs. John Greene. Dated 1769. Oil on canvas. John Singleton Copley, American. H. 49-3/8 in. 15.527

Mrs. West and Her Son Raphael. Oil on canvas. Ca. 1770. Benjamin West, American. W. 35-1/4 in. 27.393

161

Portrait of Nathaniel Hurd. Oil on canvas. Ca. 1765. John Singleton Copley, American. H. 30 in. 15.534*

Portrait of George Washington. Oil on canvas. Ca. 1790. Joseph Wright, American. H. 21 in. 2552.21

Portrait of Mrs. John Thomson Mason. Oil on canvas. Ca. 1803. Gilbert Stuart, American. H. 28-1/2 in. 21.428

Captain Jean T. David. Dated 1813. Oil on canvas. Thomas Sully, American. H. 35-1/4 in. 16.1979

Portrait of Samuel Williams. Oil on canvas. Ca. 1818. Washington Allston, American. H. 56 in. 65.474*

Marble Mantel. England, late 18th century. H. 60 in. 44.471

Chair. From a set of furniture made for the Derby family, Salem. Carved mahogany with ebony feet. Attributed to Samuel McIntire, American, Salem, Massachusetts, 1757-1811. H. 38-1/4 in. 62.125

Pair of Spurs. Silver. Paul Revere, Jr., American, Boston, 1735-1818. W. 4-1/2 in. 40.252, 40.253

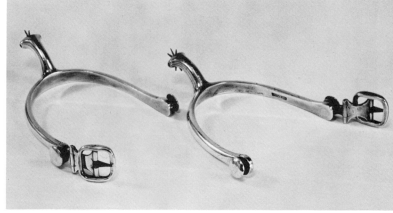

163

Plate. From a service made for Samuel Shaw. Porcelain. China, made for
the American market, late 18th century. D. 7-3/4 in. 61.178

Front Doorway. From the Isaac Gillet
House, Painesville, Ohio. Carved
and painted wood, glass and metal.
Designed by Jonathan Goldsmith,
American, Ohio, 1783-1847.
H. 9 ft. 6-1/4 in. 59.342

Centerpiece. Silver. 1808-1809. Paul Storr, English, London. H. 26 in. 43.189*

Cupid and Psyche. Dated 1817. Oil on canvas. Jacques Louis David, French. W. 95-1/8 in. 62.37*

Study of a Nude Woman, Seated Looking to the Right. Black and white chalk on blue paper. Pierre Paul Prud'hon, French, 1758-1823. H. 20-7/16 in. 61.318*

Pasture Rose (Rosa Carolina Corymbosa). Water color on vellum. Pierre Joseph Redouté, French, 1759-1840. H. 15-3/8 in. 59.15

Madame Dugazon as Andromache. Oil on canvas. Ca. 1783. Jacques Louis David, French. H. 20-1/2 in. 52.542

Terpsichore. Marble. Dated 1816. Antonio Canova, Italian. H. 69-7/8 in. 68.212

Portrait of Madame Raoul-Rochette.
Dated 1830. Pencil drawing. Jean
Auguste Dominique Ingres, French.
H. 12-11/16 in. 27.437*

Antiochus and Stratonice. Oil on canvas. 1834. Jean Auguste Dominique
Ingres, French. W. 25 in. 66.13

Fowling Piece (detail). Steel,
partially gilt, silver, walnut.
Ca. 1809. Jean Le Page, French,
Paris. Total L. 45-7/8 in. 66.433

Flower Stand. Wood and gilt bronze.
Ca. 1800. France. H. 41 in. 60.94

*Portrait of Comte Jean-Antoine
Chaptal.* Dated 1824. Oil on canvas.
Antoine Jean Gros, French.
H. 53-3/4 in. 64.54

*Portrait of the Infante Don Luis
de Borbón.* Oil on canvas. 1783-1784.
Francisco de Goya y Lucientes,
Spanish. H. 60-1/8 in. 66.14*

Portrait of Don Juan Antonio Cuervo.
Dated 1819. Oil on canvas.
Francisco de Goya y Lucientes,
Spanish. H. 47-5/16 in. 43.90*

The Garroted Man. Etching, state I/II.
Francisco de Goya y Lucientes,
Spanish, 1746-1828. H. 12-15/16 in.
63.470

Greek Pirates Attacking a Turkish Vessel. Dated 1827. Oil on canvas.
Eugène Louis Gabriel Isabey, French. W. 29-3/16 in. 16.1034

*The Bulls of Bordeaux: The
Celebrated American, Mariano
Ceballos.* Lithograph, state II/II.
Francisco de Goya y Lucientes,
Spanish, 1746-1828. W. 16-1/16 in. 49.2

Mlle. Julie de la Boutraye. Oil on canvas. 1834. Eugène Delacroix, French. H. 28-3/4 in. 62.3

Wild Horse. Dated 1828. Lithograph, state I/II. Eugène Delacroix, French. H. 9-3/8 in. 41.214

Armored Figure on Horseback. Pencil and sepia wash. Eugène Delacroix, French, 1798-1863. W. 15-11/16 in. 33.418

Halt of the Greek Cavaliers. Dated 1858. Oil on canvas. Eugène Delacroix, French. W. 24 in. 16.1032

168

Fighting Horses. Pencil and brown, blue, and black washes. Théodore Géricault, French, 1791-1824. W. 11-7/8 in. 29.13*

The Roman Campagna. Oil on canvas. 1826-1827. Jean Baptiste Camille Corot, French. W. 53-1/4 in. 63.91*

Duchess of Ragusa. Dated 1818. On vellum. Jean-Baptiste Isabey, French. H. 8-3/8 in. 42.1146

Ville d'Avray, A Peasant Cutting Reeds in a Swamp.
Oil on canvas. Jean Baptiste Camille Corot,
French, 1796-1875. W. 39 in. 44.80

Odalisque. Oil on canvas. Thomas Couture, French, 1815-1879.
W. 36-1/4 in. 39.63

Coast near Villerville. Dated 1855. Oil on canvas.
Charles François Daubigny, French. W. 45-5/8 in. 51.323

Saint Etienne-du-Mont. Etching,
state I/VIII. 1852. Charles Meryon,
French. H. 9-3/4 in. 55.528

Connoisseurs. Charcoal, pencil, and water color. Honoré Daumier, French, 1808-1879. H. 10-1/4 in. 27.208*

The Troubador. Oil on canvas. Honoré Daumier, French, 1808-1879. H. 32-3/4 in. 58.23

Madame Boreau (La Dame au chapeau noir). Dated 1863. Oil on canvas. Gustave Courbet, French. H. 31-7/8 in. 62.2*

Grand Panorama of the Alps with the Dents du Midi. Oil on canvas. Ca. 1875. Gustave Courbet, French. W. 82-11/16 in. 64.420

Mother and Children. Dated 1879. Oil on canvas. William A. Bouguereau, French. H. 64-3/4 in. 432.15

Tannhäuser. Oil on canvas. Henri Fantin-Latour, French, 1836-1904. W. 39-3/4 in. 16.1038

Summer. Dated 1891. Oil on canvas. Pierre Puvis de Chavannes, French. W. 91-1/2 in. 16.1056

Miniature Bidet. Gold, jade, enamel, pearls. Made after 1903. Firm of Carl Fabergé; Henrik Wigström, workmaster, Russian, St. Petersburg. H. 3-1/4 in. 66.455

Easter Egg. Lapis lazuli, gold, pearls, rubies, diamonds, enamel. Late 19th-early 20th century. Firm of Carl Fabergé, Russian, St. Petersburg. H. 2-5/16 in. 66.436

Bust of a Lady. Dated 1875. Terra cotta. Jules Dalou, French. H. 24-1/4 in. 67.31

Mlle. Claire Campbell. Pastel. 1875. Edouard Manet, French. H. 22-3/8 in. 56.718

Portrait of Berthe Morisot. Oil on canvas. Ca. 1869. Edouard Manet, French. H. 29 in. 58.34

Boats. Oil on canvas. 1873. Edouard Manet, French. W. 22 in. 40.534

Portrait of the Duchess of Montejasi-Cicerale. Oil on canvas. 1868. Hilaire-Germain Edgar Degas, French. H. 19-1/4 in. 58.28*

Saint-Mammès, Loing Canal. Dated 1885. Oil on canvas. Alfred Sisley, French. W. 21 in. 61.262

Portrait of Diego Martelli. Charcoal and white chalk on brown paper. 187 Hilaire-Germain Edgar Degas, French. H. 17-5/16 in. 53.268*

173

Dancer Looking at the Sole of Her Right Foot. Bronze. Hilaire-Germain Edgar Degas, French, 1834-1917. H. 18 in. 2028.47

Mlle. Romaine Lacaux. Dated 1864. Oil on canvas. Pierre Auguste Renoir, French. H. 31-7/8 in. 42.1065

Frieze of Dancers. Oil on canvas. 1883. Hilaire-Germain Edgar Degas, French. W. 79 in. 46.83*

Esterel Village. Monotype. Hilaire-Germain Edgar Degas, French, 1834-1917. W. 16-3/4 in. 66.177

The Artist's Sister, Mme. Pontillon, Seated on the Grass. Oil on canvas. 1873. Berthe Morisot, French. W. 28-1/2 in. 50.89

Spring Flowers. Dated 1864. Oil on canvas. Claude Oscar Monet, French. H. 46 in. 53.155

Le Fond de l'Hermitage. Dated 1879. Oil on canvas. Camille Pissarro, French. W. 64-1/4 in. 51.356

La Capeline Rouge–Mme. Monet. Oil on canvas. 1870-1875. Claude Oscar Monet, French. H. 39-1/2 in. 58.39

The Cowherdess, Eragny. Charcoal. Camille Pissarro, French, 1830-1903. H. 15-1/2 in. 2609.47

Ballet Girls. Pastel on paper, pasted on cardboard. Hilaire-Germain Edgar Degas, French, 1834-1917. H. 21-3/4 in. 16.1043

Race Horses. Pastel on cardboard. Ca. 1873-1875.
Hilaire-Germain Edgar Degas, French. W. 25-3/4 in.
58.27

Low Tide at Pourville near Dieppe. Dated 1882.
Claude Oscar Monet, French. W. 32 in. 47.196

The Age of Bronze. Bronze. 1876.
Auguste Rodin, French.
H. 71-3/16 in. 18.328*

William E. Henley. Bronze. 1882.
Auguste Rodin, French.
H. 16-3/8 in. 40.581

Mignon: Bust of Rose Beuret (Mme. Rodin). Bronze. Ca. 1870.
Auguste Rodin, French.
H. 16-3/16 in. 46.351

Antibes. Oil on canvas. 1888. Claude Oscar Monet, French. W. 36 in. 16.1044*

Three Bathers. Oil on canvas. 1897. Pierre Auguste Renoir, French. W. 25-7/8 in. 39.269*

The Judgment of Paris. Bronze. 1914. Pierre Auguste Renoir (and Richard Guino), French. H. 29-1/4 in. 41.591

The Apple Seller. Oil on canvas. Ca. 1890. Pierre Auguste Renoir, French. H. 25-7/8 in. 58.47

*Young Woman Arranging Her
Earrings.* Oil on canvas. 1905.
Pierre Auguste Renoir, French.
H. 21-3/4 in. 51.324

Siesta. Red chalk. Pierre Auguste
Renoir, French, 1841-1919.
H. 12-3/16 in. 49.551

The Pigeon Tower at Montbriand. Oil on canvas. Ca. 1894-1896.
Paul Cézanne, French. W. 31-1/2 in. 36.19*

The Brook. Oil on canvas. 1898-1900. Paul Cézanne, French.
W. 31-3/4 in. 58.20

La Montagne Sainte-Victoire. Oil on canvas. 1894-1900.
Paul Cézanne, French. W. 36-1/4 in. 58.21

Mademoiselle Ravoux. Oil on canvas.
1890. Vincent van Gogh, Dutch.
Sq. 19-3/4 in. 58.31

Les Baigneurs (small plate). Lithograph printed in colors.
Paul Cézanne, French, 1839-1906. W. 10-3/4 in. 63.598

The Road Menders at Arles. Oil on canvas. 1889. Vincent van Gogh,
Dutch. W. 36-1/4 in. 47.209

Poplars on a Hill. Oil on canvas.
1889-1890. Vincent van Gogh, Dutch.
H. 24 in. 58.31

Monsieur Boileau at the Café.
Gouache on cardboard. 1893.
Henri de Toulouse-Lautrec, French.
H. 31-1/2 in. 394.25*

The Laundress. Brush and black ink,
heightened with white on
scratchboard. 1888. Henri de
Toulouse-Lautrec, French. H. 30 in.
52.113

May Belfort. Oil on cardboard. 1895.
Henri de Toulouse-Lautrec, French.
H. 24-3/4 in. 58.54

Madame C. Oil on canvas.
Eugène Carrière, French, 1849-1906.
W. 18-1/8 in. 67.126

The Jockey. Dated 1899. Lithograph.
Henri de Toulouse-Lautrec, French.
H. 20-5/16 in. 67.234

180

Banks of the Seine at Suresnes. Oil on wood. 1883. Georges Seurat, French. W. 10-7/16 in. 58.51

Rodin Working on "The Gates of Hell." Bronze. Emile Antoine Bourdelle, French, 1861-1929. H. 26-7/8 in. 43.291

Café Concert. Conte crayon with touches of white. Georges Seurat, French, 1859-1891. H. 12-3/8 in. 58.344

Portrait of Mademoiselle Violette Heymann. Dated 1910. Pastel on cardboard. Odilon Redon, French. W. 36-3/8 in. 1976.26

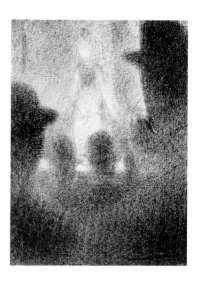

Vase of Flowers. Oil on canvas.
Ca. 1905. Odilon Redon, French.
H. 36-1/8 in. 35.233

Orpheus. Pastel on cardboard.
Odilon Redon, French, 1840-1916.
H. 27-1/2 in. 26.25*

The Slopes of the Bay, Beg-ar-Fry.
Oil on canvas. Maxime Maufra,
French, 1862-1918. W. 28-7/8 in.
66.382

Yeux Clos. Lithograph. Odilon Redon,
French, 1840-1916. H. 12-5/16 in.
27.306

L'Appel. Dated 1902. Oil on canvas.
Paul Gauguin, French. H. 51-1/4 in.
43.392*

Head of a Tahitian Woman. Pencil.
Paul Gauguin, French, 1848-1903.
H. 12-1/16 in. 49.439*

The Café Wepler. Oil on canvas. Ca. 1905.
Edouard Vuillard, French. W. 40-5/8 in. 50.90

Street Scene. Pastel on paper. Maurice de Vlaminck,
French, 1876-1958. W. 21-1/4 in. 66.378

Under the Trees. Dated 1894.
Tempera on canvas. Edouard
Vuillard, French. H. 84-1/2 in.
53.212

La Porte de Saint-Cloud. Dated 1904. Oil on canvas. Pierre Albert Marquet,
French. W. 32 in. 61.263

General Duncan Campbell. Oil on canvas. Ca. 1806. Sir Henry Raeburn, English. H. 30 in. 47.266

Burning of the Houses of Parliament, 1834. Oil on canvas. 1835. Joseph Mallord William Turner, English. W. 48-1/2 in. 42.647*

Fluelen–Lake of Lucerne. Water color. Joseph Mallord Turner, English, 1775-1851. W. 18-3/4 in. 54.129

The Lonely Tower. Etching, state I/VI. 1879. Samuel Palmer, English. W. 9-1/8 in. 66.199

A Hussar Officer on Horseback.
Black and white chalk on blue paper.
John Singleton Copley, American,
1737-1815. H. 10-13/16 in. 50.216

The Peaceable Kingdom. Oil on canvas.
1830. Edward Hicks, American.
W. 23-1/2 in. 45.38

The Devil and Tom Walker. Dated
1856. Oil on canvas. John Quidor,
American. W. 34-3/8 in. 67.18

Schroon Mountain, The Adirondacks. Dated 1833. Oil
on canvas. Thomas Cole, American. W. 63 in. 1335.17

View of Florence from San Miniato. Oil on canvas. 1837.
Thomas Cole, American. W. 63-1/8 in. 61.39

View near Newport. Oil on canvas. Ca. 1860. John Frederick Kensett, American. W. 22 in. 46.255

October Day in the White Mountains. Dated 1854. Oil on canvas. John Frederick Kensett, American. W. 48-3/8 in. 67.5

Twilight in the Wilderness. Dated 1860. Oil on canvas. Frederick Edwin Church, American. W. 64 in. 65.233*

Portrait of Gineo Scott. Dated 1859. Oil on canvas. Eastman Johnson, American. W. 50 in. 65.475

The Venetian Girl. Oil on canvas. Frank Duveneck, American, 1848-1919. H. 34 in. 22.173

Approaching Storm from Alban Hills. Dated 187(?). Oil on canvas. George Inness, American. W. 44-1/2 in. 27.396

The Balcony. Etching, state I/XI. James McNeill Whistler, American, 1834-1903. H. 11-5/8 in. 40.1088

Boy with the Anchor. Dated 1873. Water color on paper pasted on composition board. Winslow Homer, American. W. 13-3/4 in. 54.128

High Tide on the Marshes. Oil on canvas. Martin Johnson Heade, American, 1819-1904. W. 30-1/8 in. 490.15

The Briarwood Pipe. Dated 1864.
Oil on canvas. Winslow Homer,
American. H. 16-7/8 in. 44.524

Early Morning After a Storm at Sea. Oil on canvas. 1902. Winslow Homer,
American. W. 50 in. 24.195

Biglen Brothers Turning the Stake. Dated 1873. Oil on
canvas. Thomas Eakins, American. W. 60-1/4 in. 1984.27*

The Clambake. Dated 1873. Water color on paper.
Winslow Homer, American. W. 13-7/8 in. 45.229

Rishi Calling up a Storm. Water color. John La Farge, American, 1835-1910. W. 12-7/8 in. 39.267

The Race Track, or Death on a Pale Horse. Oil on canvas. Ca. 1910. Albert Pinkham Ryder, American. W. 35-1/4 in. 28.8*

Portrait of Miss Dora Wheeler. Oil on canvas. 1883. William Merritt Chase, American. W. 65-1/4 in. 21.1239

After the Bath. Pastel. Ca. 1901. Mary Cassatt, American. W. 39-1/4 in. 20.379

The Visitor. Soft ground etching and aquatint, state II/V. Mary Cassatt, American, 1845-1926. H. 15-3/4 in. 66.176

Window. Glass. Ca. 1900-1901. Louis Comfort Tiffany, American. H. 89-1/2 in. 66.432

Fifth Avenue Nocturne. Oil on canvas. Ca. 1895. Childe Hassam, American. H. 24-1/8 in. 52.538

May Day, Central Park. Dated 1901. Water color. Maurice Prendergast, American. W. 19-3/4 in. 26.17

Building a Dam, Shetucket. Oil on canvas. 1908. J. Alden Weir, American. W. 40-1/4 in. 27.171

The Drive, Central Park. Oil on canvas. Ca. 1905. William J. Glackens, American. W. 32 in. 39.524

Self Portrait (George Bellows Drawing on a Stone in His Study). Lithograph. 1921. George Wesley Bellows, American. H. 10-1/2 in. 35.279

Stag at Sharkey's. Oil on canvas. 1907. George Wesley Bellows, American. W. 48-1/4 in. 1133.22

Holiday on the Hudson. Oil on canvas. Ca. 1912. George Benjamin Luks, American. W. 36-1/8 in. 2291.33

Still Life. Oil on canvas. Preston Dickinson, American, 1891-1930. W. 30-1/8 in. 1664.26

Church Bells Ringing, Rainy Winter Night. Dated 1917. Water color. Charles E. Burchfield, American. H. 30 in. 49.544

Woman's Work. Oil on canvas. John Sloan, American, 1871-1951. H. 31-5/8 in. 64.160

The Sunflower Arch. Dated 1917. Indelible pencil and crayon. Charles E. Burchfield, American. H. 19-7/8 in. 65.461

Fireworks. Dated 1926. Water color. George Overbury ("Pop") Hart, American. W. 27-3/4 in. 38.125

Hills, South Truro. Oil on canvas. 1930.
Edward Hopper, American. W. 43-1/8 in. 2647.31

Houses in Old Paris. Woodcut. 1919.
Lyonel Feininger, American.
H. 12-5/16 in. 52.27

Markwippach III. Dated 1916. Charcoal.
Lyonel Feininger, American. W. 10-1/16 in. 63.73

The Motor Boat. Oil on canvas. Dated 1931. Lyonel Feininger, American.
W. 30-1/2 in. 64.53

Landscape, New Mexico. Oil on canvas. Marsden Hartley, American, 1878-1943. W. 35-3/4 in. 30.665

Rock and Sea, Small Point, Maine. Dated 1931. Oil on canvas. John Marin, American. W. 27-15/16 in. 56.361

Markwippach. Oil on canvas. 1917. Lyonel Feininger, American. W. 39-3/4 in. 60.180

Storm-frightened Animals. Oil on canvas. 1933. Henry G. Keller, American. W. 40 in. 34.56

Mountain Top. Water color. John Marin, American, 1870-1953. W. 19-1/2 in. 2731.30

Wounded Scoter, No. 2. Water color on rice paper mounted on cloth. 1944. Morris Graves, American. W. 29-7/8 in. 45.231

Horses in Snow. Water color. Ca. 1933. William Sommer, American. W. 21-1/2 in. 33.24

Deserted Farm. Oil on canvas. 1943. Max Weber, American. W. 48-1/2 in. 210.46

Woman with Cape. Oil on canvas. Ca. 1901. Pablo Picasso, Spanish. H. 28-3/4 in. 58.44

La Vie. Oil on canvas. 1903. Pablo Picasso, Spanish. H. 77-3/8 in. 45.24

The Donkey Driver. Dated 1902. Pencil. Pablo Picasso, Spanish. H. 10-5/16 in. 58.12

Head of a Boy. Gouache. 1905. Pablo Picasso, Spanish. H. 12-3/16 in. 58.43

Reclining Nude. Gouache. 1905. Pablo Picasso, Spanish. W. 24-1/8 in. 54.865

Figures in Pink. Oil on canvas. 1905. Pablo Picasso, Spanish (French School) H. 60-3/4 in. 58.45

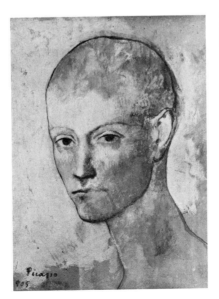

196

Melancholia: On the Beach. Woodcut colored by hand. 1896. Edvard Munch, Norwegian. W. 17-11/16 in. 59.82

Karneval Im Schnee. Water color. 1923. Paul Klee, German (born in Switzerland). H. 10-1/2 in. 69.46

Still Life: Fan, Salt Box, and Melon. Oil on canvas. 1909. Pablo Picasso, Spanish (French School). W. 32 in. 69.22

Wrestlers in a Circus. Oil on canvas. Ca. 1909. Ernst Ludwig Kirchner, German. W. 37 in. 66.49

Le Violoncelle. Oil on chipboard. Ca. 1912-1913. Georges Braque, French, 1882-1963. H. 28-1/4 in. 68.196

Torso. Brass. 1917. Constantin Brancusi, Romanian (French School). H. 18-3/8 in. 3205.37

Self Portrait with Hat. Oil on canvas. 1919. Karl Schmidt-Rottluff, German. H. 28-7/8 in 65.440

Water Lilies. Oil on canvas. 1919-1926. Claude Monet, French. W. 13 ft. 11-1/2 in. 60.81

Mountain Landscape with Fir Trees. Pencil and brush and India ink. Ernst Ludwig Kirchner, German, 1880-1938. W. 20-15/16 in. 63.86

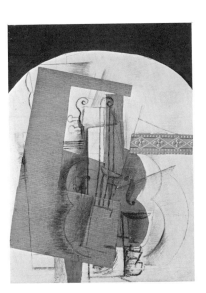

198

Landscape. Oil on canvas. 1943. Arshile Gorky, American.
W. 25 in. 63.152.

Mother and Child. Bronze. 1929-1930.
Jacques Lipchitz, American.
H. 51-1/4 in. 55.166

The Wounded Soldier. Oil on canvas.
1930. José Clemente Orozco, Mexican.
H. 44-1/4 in. 54.864

Composition with Red, Yellow, and Blue. Oil on canvas. 1927.
Piet Mondrian, Dutch, 1872-1944.
H. 20-1/8 in. 67.215

Head of Christ. Oil on canvas. 1938.
Georges Rouault, French.
H. 41-1/4 in. 50.399

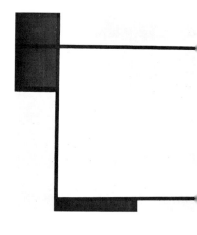

199

Carnival at Nice. Oil on canvas. Henri Matisse, French, 1869-1954. W. 37-1/2 in. 46.444

Potager à la Brunié. Oil on canvas. 1941. Jacques Villon, French. W. 36-1/4 in. 64.95

Interior with Etruscan Vase. Oil on canvas. 1940. Henri Matisse, French. W. 42-1/2 in. 52.153*

Constellation: Woman with Blond Armpit Combing Her Hair by the Light of the Stars. Oil and gouache on paper. 1940. Joan Miró, Spanish. W. 18-1/8 in. 65.2*

Madonna and Child. Pen and ink wash. 1943. Henry Spencer Moore, English. H. 8-7/8 in. 313.47

Mallarmé's Swan. Collage with gouache, crayon, and paper on cardboard. 1944. Robert Motherwell, American. H. 43-1/2 in. 61.229*

Woman and Bird. Oil on canvas. 1944. Rufino Tamayo, Mexican. H. 42 in. 50.583

Figure. Oil on cardboard. 1949. Willem de Kooning, American (born in Holland). H. 18-3/8 in. 64.1

Fragmented Figure Construction. Welded steel. 1963. Richard Hunt, American. H. 56-1/2 in. 69.16

Lom-Lan. Oil on canvas. 1949-1952. Victor Vasarely, Hungarian (French School). H. 36-3/16 in. 65.427

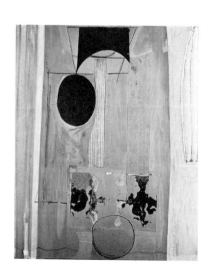

Mandrake. Steel brazed with copper. 1951. Theodore Roszak, American (born in Poland). W. 40 in. 64.4

Video. Construction of mixed media. Joseph Cornell, American. W. 14-1/2 in. 64.143

Pilgrim. Steel. 1957. David Smith, American. H. 81-1/2 in. 66.385

Woman with Child. Marble. 1958. Isamu Noguchi, American. H. 43-1/2 in. 66.48

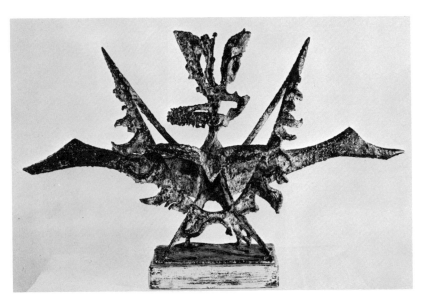

Sleeper I. Oil on canvas. 1958. Philip Guston, American (born in Canada). W. 76 in. 61.21

Accent Grave. Oil on canvas. 1955. Franz Kline, American. H. 75-1/4 in. 67.3

Crest. Oil on canvas. 1957. Jack Tworkov, American (born in Poland). H. 75 in. 62.33

Elegy to the Spanish Republic No. LV. Oil on canvas. 1955-1960. Robert Motherwell, American. W. 76-1/8 in. 63.583

Smaragd Red and Germinating Yellow. Oil on canvas. 1959. Hans Hofmann, American (born in Germany). H. 55 in. 60.57

203

Red Maroons. Oil on canvas. 1962. Mark Rothko, American (born in Russia). W. 81 in. 62.239*

Composition Concrete (Study for Mural). Oil on canvas. 1957-1960. Stuart Davis, American. H. 42-3/4 in. 64.2

Red Blue. Oil on canvas. 1962. Ellsworth Kelly, American. H. 90 in. 64.142

Gloria. Oil and paper collage on canvas. 1956. Robert Rauschenberg, American. H. 66-1/4 in. 66.333

Louis II. Oil on canvas. 1962. Richard Lindner, American (born in Germany). H. 50 in. 65.450

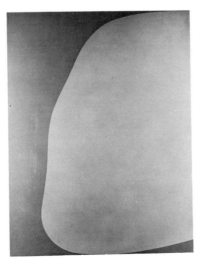

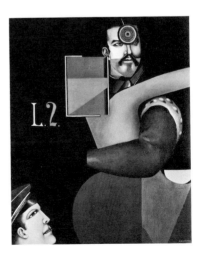

Untitled. Acrylic on canvas. 1969.
Larry Poons, American. H. 135 in.
69.49

Number 99. Acrylic on canvas. 1959. Morris Louis,
American. W. 142 in. 68.110

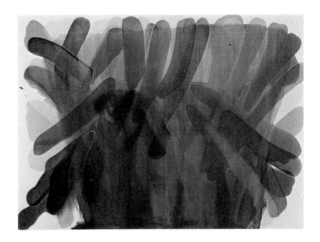

Notes

Notes

Islamic Art

Gold Ewer. Repoussé and engraved. Iran, Buyid Period, reign of Samsam al-Dawla (985-998). H. 4-3/4 in. 66.22

Tombstone. Marble. Iran, Seljuk Period, 1110. H. 25-3/8 in. 50.9

Hitching Post. Limestone. Iran, Seljuk Period, 13th century. H. 24-3/4 in. 44.481

End of Balustrade. Limestone. Iran, Hamadan, Mongol Period, 1304. H. 26-1/4 in. 38.15

Lion Incense Burner. Bronze, cast and engraved. Iran, Seljuk Period, 12th century. H. 14-1/8 in. 48.308

Bird-shaped Vessel. Bronze, cast and engraved, with turquoise eyes. Iran, Seljuk Period, 12th-13th century. H. 6-7/8 in. 48.458

Ewer. Dated 1223. Brass, inlaid with silver. Made by Ahmad al-Dhaki, al-Naqsh, al-Mawsili, Iraqi (Mesopotamia), Mosul. H. 15 in. 56.11

Footed Bowl. Bronze, inlaid with silver. Iran, Seljuk Period, early 13th century. H. 4-1/2 in. 44.485

Tray. Brass, inlaid with silver. Syria, mid-13th century. D. 21-1/4 in. 45.386

Candlestick. Brass, inlaid with silver and engraved. Syria, 13th century. H. 9-3/4 in. 51.539

210

Box. Bronze, inlaid with gold and silver. Syria, 13th century. H. 3-7/8 in. 44.482

Bowl. Enameled glass. Egypt or Syria, Mamluke Period, 14th century. D. 12-1/2 in. 44.235

Pottery Bowl. Luster ware. Egypt, Fustat, 11th century. D. 10 in. 44.476

Bottle. Enameled glass, Egypt or Syria, Mamluke Period, 14th century. H. 17-5/16 in. 44.488

Pottery Bowl. Polychrome painted ware. Iran, Nishapur, 10th century. D. 11 in. 56.225

Pottery Bowl. Polychrome painted ware. Iran, Nishapur, 10th century. D. 14 in. 59.249*

Pottery Bowl. Lakabi ware. Iran, 11th-12th century. D. 16 in. 38.7*

Pottery Bowl. Champlevé ware. Iran, Garruz district, 11th-12th century. D. 15-3/8 in. 38.8

Pottery Jug. Underglaze slip-painted ware. Iran, 12th century. H. 5-1/4 in. 47.495

Pottery Plate. Luster ware. Iran, Gurgan, 12th-13th century. D. 15-1/2 in. 51.289

Pottery Bottle. Luster ware. Iran, Rayy, 12th-13th century. H. 13-15/16 in. 15.525

Pottery Bowl. Minai ware. Iran, Rayy, early 13th century. D. 8-1/4 in. 39.214

Pottery Wall Tile. Luster ware. Iran, Kashan, 1266. H. 8 in. 15.524

Pottery Beaker. Minai ware. Iran, Rayy, early 13th century. H. 5-3/8 in. 17.977

Mihrab and Frieze. Faïence mosaic tiles. Iran, Isfahan, 1st half 16th century. H. 114-1/2 in. 62.23*

Textile Panel. Tapestry weave, wool and linen. Egypt, Abbasid Period, 1st half 9th century. H. 31-1/2 in. 59.48*

Tiraz. Silk and gold tapestry on linen. Egypt, Fatimid Period, reign of Musta'li, 1094-1101. Over-all: H. 21-1/2 in. Detail: H. 7-1/2 in. 65.313

Tiraz. Tapestry weave, silk on linen. Egypt, Fatimid Period, reign of Mustanzir, 1036-1094. Over-all: 15-1/2 in. Detail: H. 7-1/2 in. 50.528

Textile. Tapestry weave, silk and gold on linen. Egypt, Fatimid Period, late 11th century. H. 6-1/2 in. 50.541

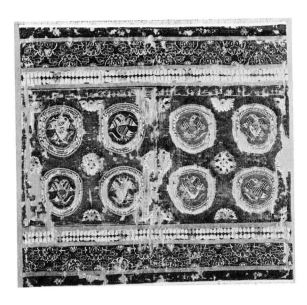

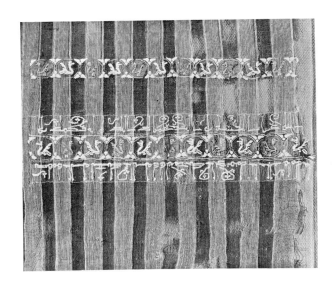

Textile. Tapestry weave, silk and linen. Egypt, Fatimid Period, 1st half 12th century. H. 5-1/8 in. 52.255

Textile. Diasper weave, silk. Egypt, Ayyubid Period, 12th century. H. 13-1/4 in. 37.23

Textile. Embroidery, silk and gold on *mulham.* Egypt or Sicily, 12th century. Over-all: W. 8-1/2 in. Detail: H. 2-7/8 in. 50.533

Textile. Diasper weave, silk and gold. Egypt, Mamluke Period, 14th century. Over-all: W. 43-3/4 in. Detail: H. 27-1/2 in. 39.40

Textile. Printed on *mulham.* Iraq (Mesopotamia), 10th century. Over-all: W. 15-3/4 in. Detail: H. 10-1/2 in. 50.558

Tomb Cover. Compound twill, silk.
Iran, Buyid Period, 10th century.
H. 82-3/4 in. 54.780

Fragment of a Tomb Cover.
Compound twill, silk. Iran, Buyid
Period, 998. H. 30-3/4 in. 55.52*

Part of a Textile Panel. Diasper weave, silk. Iran, Buyid Period, 1003.
W. 37-1/8 in. 61.34

Textile Panel. Diasper weave, silk.
Iran, Buyid Period, 10th-11th century.
H. 67-3/8 in. 62.264*

Textile. Diasper weave, silk. Iran,
Buyid Period, 10th-11th century.
Over-all: W. 17-1/2 in. Detail:
H. 12 in. 50.84

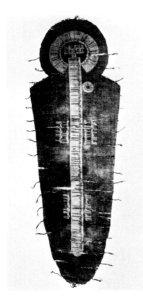

216

Textile. Diasper weave, silk. Iran,
Buyid Period, 10th-11th century.
Over-all: H. 18-3/4 in. Detail:
H. 10-1/2 in. 53.434

Textile. Velvet weave, silk and gold.
Iran, Safavid Period, reign of Shah
Tahmasp, 1524-1576. H. 27-1/2 in.
48.205

Textile. Soumak weave, silk. Iran,
Seljuk Period, 11th-12th century.
H. 7-7/8 in. 39.47

Textile. Diasper weave, silk. Iran,
Herat, Safavid Period, early 16th
century. H. 32-7/8 in. 24.743

Textile. Velvet weave, silk. Iran,
Safavid Period, 2nd half 16th century.
H. 12-1/4 in. (as mounted). 44.499,
44.500

217

Fragment of a Carpet. Senna knot, wool and cotton, Iran, Safavid Period, 16th century. Over-all: W. 73 in. Detail: H. 33-1/2 in. 53.128

Textile. Velvet weave, silk and gold. Iran, Safavid Period, 16th century. Over-all: H. 30-1/2 in. Detail: H. 21 in. 44.239

Carpet. Senna knot, wool and cotton. Iran, Herat, Safavid Period, 16th century. Over-all: H. 25 ft. 4 in. Detail: H. 22 ft. 8 in. 62.263

Carpet. Senna knot, silk and cotton. Iran, Isfahan, Safavid Period, ca. 1600. H. 81-1/4 in. 26.533

Textile. Velvet weave, silk and gold. Iran, Safavid Period, 17th century. H. 61-1/8 in. 32.42*

Textile. Diasper weave, silk and gold. Iran, Safavid Period, 17th century. Over-all: H. 34-1/2 in. Detail: H. 22 in. 53.17

218

Textile. Diasper weave, silk and gold. Spain, Almeria, 12th century. H. 14-3/8 in. 52.15

Textile. Compound twill, silk. Spain, 11th-12th century. Over-all: W. 40-1/4 in. Detail: H. 20-5/8 in. 51.92

Textile. Compound weave, silk and gold. Spain, Almeria, 13th century. H. 6-1/2 in. 32.137

Textile. Diasper weave, silk and gold. Spain, Almeria, 12th century. H. 17 in. 50.146*

Textile. Compound weave, silk and gold. Spain, Almeria, 13th century. H. 3-7/8 in. 42.1077

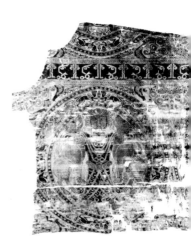

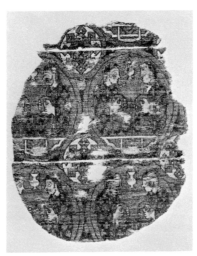

219

Textile. Tapestry weave, silk and gold. Spain, 13th century. H. 6-7/8 in. 52.105

Textile. Diasper weave, silk and gold. Spain, 13th century. Over-all: H. 27 in. Detail: H. 13-1/2 in. 52.106

Textile. Tapestry weave, silk and gold. Spain, Almeria, 13th century. Over-all: H. 10-1/4 in. Detail: H. 2-3/8 in. 28.650

Textile. Compound weave, silk, linen, and gold. Spain, Burgos, 13th century. H. 9-3/4 in. 50.4

220

Textile. Diasper weave, silk and gold. Spain, Granada, 14th century. H. 18-3/4 in. 39.35

Textile. Diasper weave, silk. Spain, Granada, 14th century. H. 30-1/4 in. 46.417

Textile. Diasper weave, silk. Spain, Granada, 14th century. Over-all: H. 20 in. Detail: H. 15-3/4 in. 40.609

Textile. Diasper weave, silk. Spain, Granada, 15th century. Over-all: H. 22-3/4 in. Detail: H. 12-1/2 in. 29.83

Carpet. Single knot, wool. Spain, Alcarez(?), 2nd half 15th century. Over-all: H. 13 ft. 9 in. Detail: H. 9 ft. 52.511

221

Illustration from a Manuscript of the Automata by Al-Jazari: Device for Washing Hands. Miniature painting. Iraq (Mesopotamia), 1315. H. 12-3/8 in. 45.383

Illustration from a Manuscript of the Shahnamah of Firdawsi: Nushirwan's Fifth Banquet for Buzurdjmir. Miniature painting. Iran, Tabriz, Mongol Period, 1330-1340. H. 9-1/2 in. 59.330

Illustration from a Manuscript of the Shahnamah of Firdawsi: Bahram Gur Slays a Dragon. Miniature painting. Iran, Tabriz School (?), Mongol Period, ca. 1330-1340. H. 7-3/4 in. 43.658*

222

Double-page Frontispiece from a Manuscript of the Shahnamah of Firdawsi: Courtly Scene. Miniature painting. Iran, Shiraz, Timurid Period, ca. 1444. H. 10-1/2 in. 45.169, 56.10*

Garden Scene. Miniature painting (unfinished). Iran, Herat, Timurid Period, style of Bihzad, late 15th century. H. 10-3/8 in. 44.490

A Picnic in the Mountains. Line drawing with color. Iran, Tabriz, Safavid Period, style of Muhammadi, ca. 1550. H. 10-7/16 in. 44.491

Illustration from a Manuscript of the Shahnamah of Firdawsi: Rustam meets the Challenge of Ashkabus. Miniature painting. Iran, Timurid Period, 15th century. H. 12-13/16 in. 60.199

Ruler Seated in a Garden. Drawing with wash. Iran, Safavid Period, 16th century. H. 8-1/4 in. 39.508

223

Illustration from the Khamsa of Nizami: An Episode from the Story of Khusraw and Shirin. Miniature painting. Iran, Safavid Period, 16th century. H. 8-1/2 in. 47.500

Camel with Attendant. Drawing with wash. Safavid Period, mid-16th century. Attributed to Sultan Muhammad, Iranian. H. 8 in. 44.489

Illustration from the Khamsa of Nizami: Nushirwan and the Owls. Miniature painting. Iran, Safavid Period, 16th century. H. 8-1/2 in. 44.487

Youth Sleeping Under a Willow Tree. Miniature painting. Iran, Safavid Period, late 16th century. H. 8-3/16 in. 44.494

Illustration from a Manuscript: Courtly Procession. Miniature painting. Iran, Safavid Period, ca. 1600. Detail: H. 11 in. 62.24

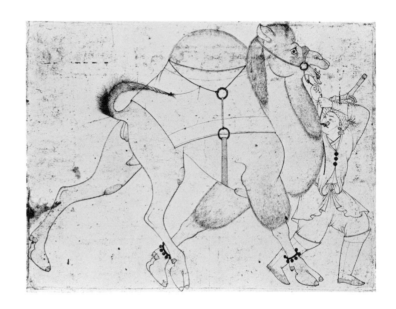

224

Dragon Combat. Drawing. Turkey, 15th century. H. 6-7/8 in. 44.492

Youth with Toy. Miniature painting.
Iran, early 17th century.
H. 10-1/2 in. 47.497

Bookbinding. Leather, chased and perforated over gold. Iran, 15th century.
H. 14-1/8 in. 44.495

Notes

Notes

Far Eastern Art

Male Head with Turban. Red
sandstone. India, Shunga Period,
185-72 B.C. H. 19 in. 62.45*

Pendant with Deity Hariti. Gold and carnelian. India, Sirkap, Saka-Parthian
Period, ca. 50 B.C.-A.D. 50. D. 2-7/8 in. 53.14

Seated Buddha. Gray schist. India,
Gandhara, 3rd century. H. 51 in.
61.418*

Bacchanalian Scene. Schist. India, Gandhara, from Buner,
1st-2nd century. W. 17 in. 30.329

Bodhisattva. Gray schist. India, Gandhara, 3rd century. H. 52-1/8 in. 65.476

Adoring Attendant. From a Buddhist shrine. Stucco. Hadda (Afghanistan), 5th century. H. 21-1/2 in. 43.395

Attendant Holding a Fly-whisk, (Chauri Bearer). Red sandstone. India, Mathura, Kushan Period, 2nd century. H. 22 in. 65.472

Standing Bodhisattva Maitreya. Red sandstone. India, Mathura, Kushan Period, 3rd century. H. 26-1/2 in. 43.661

Lion. Red sandstone. India, Mathura, Kushan Period, 1st-2nd century. H. 18-1/2 in. 52.514

Seated Ascetics. Two terra-cotta plaques. Harwan, Kashmir, 4th century. H. 20 in. 59.131, 59.132

Yakshi. Red sandstone. India, Mathura, Kushan Period, 2nd century. H. 50-1/2 in. 68.104

Head of Buddha. Red sandstone. India, Mathura, Gupta Period, 4th-5th century. H. 12 in. 63.504*

Scene of Worship (Fragment of Casing Slab). Marble. India, Nagarjunakonda, Satavahana Dynasty, late 2nd-early 3rd century. H. 23-1/4 in. 43.72

Seated Buddha. Red sandstone. India, Mathura, Proto-Gupta style, late 3rd century. H. 24 in. 41.94

Standing Buddha. Cream sandstone. India, Gupta Period, from Sarnath, 5th century. H. 30 in. 43.278

Buddha. Dated A.D. 662. Bronze. India, Gupta Period. H. 18-1/8 in. 68.40

Head of Vishnu. Red sandstone. India, Gupta Period, 5th century. H. 11 in. 42.498

Ganga, Goddess of the Ganges. Stone. India, Mathura(?), early 7th century. H. 42-1/2 in. 66.119

Standing Vishnu. Stone. India, Mathura, Gupta Period, ca. 600. H. 43 in. 63.580

Surya, the Sun God. Brass. Kashmir, early 8th century. H. 19-13/16 in. 65.557

232

Standing Buddha. Brass. North India
or Kashmir, early 8th century.
H. 38-5/8 in. 66.30*

*Buddha Calling on the Earth to
Witness.* Black chlorite. India,
Bengal, Pala Dynasty, 9th century.
H. 37 in. 35.146*

Chakrapurusa: Angel of the Discus.
Black chlorite. India, Apshad, Pala
Dynasty, ca. 670. H. 30-1/4 in.
45.367

*Bodhisattva Manjushri, (Lord of
Wisdom).* Image of gilded copper;
pedestal and mandorla of brass.
India, Bengal, Pala Dynasty, 11th-
12th century. H. 12-1/4 in. 60.285

Shiva and Parvati: Umamaheshvara.
Bronze. India, Bengal, Pala Dynasty,
reign of Devapala, 815-854. H. 7 in.
64.50*

233

*Vishnu Attended by Chakrapurusa
and Shankhapurusa.* Bronze with
silver inlay. India, Bengal, Pala
Dynasty, ca. 12th century.
H. 17-1/8 in. 64.453

Vasudhara: Goddess of Abundance.
Copper gilt with inlaid gems. Nepal,
14th-15th century. H. 6-3/8 in.
47.493

Gandavyuha: Structure of the World (detail). Illuminated
manuscript, ink and color on palm leaf. India, Bengal,
Pala Dynasty, 11th-12th century. W. 20-5/8 in. 55.49

*Astasahasrika Prajnaparamita: Book of Transcendental
Wisdom* (detail). Illuminated manuscript, color on wood
and palm leaf. Nepal, 1100. W. 22-1/8 in. 38.301

Manjushri, Bodhisattva of Wisdom.
Gilt copper. Nepal, 16th century.
H. 16-11/16 in. 56.8

Dancing Ganesha. Red sandstone.
India, Khajuraho Region, 1000.
H. 24-1/8 in. 61.93

Bodhisattva Manjushri Jananasathva.
Gilt bronze. Nepal, late 16th
century. H. 30-3/4 in. 64.370*

Mithuna (Loving Couple). Stone.
India, Rajasthan, from Harsagiri,
973. H. 13-7/8 in. 62.165

Vajravarahi: Dancing Tantric Deity.
Dry lacquer. Nepal, 16th-17th
century. H. 25 in. 64.103

Salabhanjika Figure. Stone. India,
Rajasthan, late 10th century.
H. 21-1/2 in. 67.202

Vaishnava Trinity: Shri Devi, Vishnu, Bhu Devi. Granite. India, probably from Region of Pudokkatai, early Chola Period, 1st half 10th century. H. (Vishnu) 69-1/4 in. 63.104-63.106*

Shiva and Parvati: Uma-sahitamurti. Copper. South India, early Chola Period, early 10th century. H. 40-3/4 in. 61.94*

Shiva Nataraja. Copper. South India, Chola Period, 11th century. H. 43-7/8 in. 30.331*

Gajasura-samharamurti: Shiva in Elephant-killing Aspect. South India, Chola Period, 11th century. H. 28-1/2 in. 62.164

Shiva and Parvati: Alingana-Chandrasekharamurti. Copper. South India, Chola Period, 11th-12th century. H. 13-3/8 in. 54.7

236

Shaiva Saint: Manikkavachakar.
Bronze. South India, 12th-13th
century. H. 13-3/16 in. 67.148

A Guardian of Shiva. Stone. India,
Hoysala Dynasty, Mysore, 12th
century. H. 44-5/8 in. 64.369*

*Manuscript of the Tuti-Nama by Ziya
al-din Nakhshabi: fol. 110v, A Poet-
Musician.* Color and gold on paper
(manuscript almost complete). India,
Mughal School, early reign of Akbar,
ca. 1560. H. 8 in. 62.279*

*A Young Ascetic Walking by the Bank
of a River.* Color on paper.
Attributed to Basawan, Indian, Mughal
School, ca. 1560. Over-all H. 15-5/16
in. Detail: H. 5-3/4 in. 67.244

King Parikshit and Rishis. Color on paper. India, Rajasthan, Mewar School,
ca. 1550. H. 8-9/16 in. 60.53

Siege of Arbela. Color on paper with gold. Designed by Basawan, painted by Sur Gujarati, Indian, Mughal School, late 16th century. H. 15-1/4 in. 47.502

Page from a Razm Nama. Dated 1616. Color on paper. India, Mughal School H. 13-15/16 in. 60.44

Page from Ta'rikh-i-alfi (History of a Thousand Years). Color on paper. India, Mughal School, late 16th century. H. 16-5/8 in. 32.36

Hunting Scene. Color on paper. India, Mughal School, early 17th century. H. 14-5/8 in. 39.66

Imperial Rooster. Color on paper. Signed: Dilaram Padarat Kashmiri. Indian, Mughal School, early 17th century. H. 7-3/16 in. 44.501

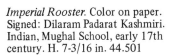

*Nayika Madhya Dhira Adhira: Page
from Bhanu Datta's Rasamanjari.*
Color on paper. India, Rajasthan,
Mewar School, ca. 1630. H. 10 in.
60.52

Ragini Kedara. Color on paper. India,
Malwa School, ca. 1680. H. 8 in.
60.116

Ragini Madhu Madhavi. Color on paper.
India, Malwa School, ca. 1660.
H. 7-7/8 in. 25.1336

Ragini Pancham. Color on paper. India,
Rajasthan, Mewar School, mid-17th
century. H. 14-9/16 in. 31.451

Krishna: Page from Rasikapriya.
Dated 1634. Color on paper. India,
Malwa School. H. 8-3/16 in. 38.303

*Shiva and Parvati Seated on an
Elephant Skin.* Color on paper. India,
Punjab Hills, Basohli School,
ca. 1700. H. 9-1/8 in. 52.587

Durga Slaying Mahisha. Color on paper. India, Punjab Hills, Basohli School, ca. 1700. W. 9-1/4 in. 60.51

Sita in the Garden of Lanka with Ravana and His Demons: The Siege of Lanka Sequence, from The Ramayana. Gold and color on paper. India, Punjab Hills, Guler School, ca. 1720. W. 33-1/4 in. 66.143*

Angry Heroine. Color on paper. India, Basohli School, ca. 1720. W. 11-1/16 in. 67.239

Raja Smoking with Son and a Courtier. Color on paper. North India, Punjab Hills, Jammu School, ca. 1730. W. 12-3/16 in. 60.47

Krishna Awaiting Radha. Color on paper. India, Punjab Hills, Guler School, ca. 1760. H. 7-5/16 in. 36.685

Toilette of Radha. Color and gold on paper. India, Punjab Hills, Kangra School, early 19th century. H. 9-1/8 in. 53.245

Palace Ladies Hunting from a Pavilion. Color and gold on paper. India, Rajasthan, Kotah School, ca. 1760-1770. H. 15 in. 55.48*

Pendant: Krishna with Devotees. Gold with enamel in champlevé technique. India, Rajasthan, 17th-18th century. H. 2 in. 46.257

Durga Slaying Mahisha. Color on paper. India, Punjab Hills, Kangra School, late 18th century. H. 10-13/16 in. 55.667

Carpet. Senna knot, silk. India, Mughal School, early 17th century, Over-all: H. 9 ft. 7-1/4 in. Detail: H. 47 in. 36.17

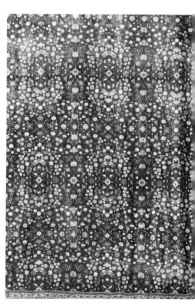

Textile. Diasper weave, silk. India, Rajput, Jaipur School, 17th century. Over-all: W. 67-7/8 in. Detail: H. 36-1/2 in. 53.474

Vishnu. Gray sandstone. Cambodia, Pre-Angkorean Period, style of Prasat Andet, 2nd half 7th century. H. 34-1/4 in. 42.562*

Head of Buddha. Bluish-gray sandstone. Cambodia, Pre-Angkorean Period, style of Tra Vinh, late 6th-early 7th century. H. 10 in. 32.43

Head of Shiva. Tan sandstone. Cambodia, Koh Ker style, reign of Jayavarman IV, 928-941. H. 16-1/2 in. 40.53*

Buddha with Hands in Gesture of Teaching, Vitarka Mudra. Bronze. Thailand, Mon Dvaravati Period, 7th century. H. 8-1/4 in. 58.334

Rakshasa. Gray sandstone. Cambodia, Koh Ker style, 10th century. H. 27-1/2 in. 67.146

Shiva. Gray sandstone. Cambodia, style of Baphuon, 1st half 11th century. H. 30-1/4 in. 41.25

Buddha Enthroned. Bronze altarpiece. Cambodia, Angkor Wat style, ca. 1112-1153. H. 10-1/2 in. 42.149

Lintel with Garuda and Three-headed Naga. Sandstone. Cambodia, 9th-10th century. H. 20-11/16 in. 67.37

Finial: Buddha Calling on the Earth to Witness. Bronze. Cambodia, ca. 1200. H. 15-7/16 in. 64.93

Buddha Sheltered by Mucalinda, the Serpent King. Bronze. Cambodia, Period of Angkor Wat, early 12th century. H. 23 in. 63.263*

Lokeshvara. Sandstone. Cambodia, reign of Jayavarman VII, Second Angkorean Period, 1002-1201. H. 13-1/8 in. 55.47

243

Princess. From the Terrace of the
Leper King Angkor Thom. Sandstone.
Cambodia, reign of Jayavarman VII,
ca. 1181-1218. H. 24 in. 38.304

Shiva. Sandstone. Viet Nam, Champa,
from Dong-duong, Indrapura, 9th
century. H. 34 in. 35.147

Dancing Apsaras: Heavenly Beings. Section of a lintel from the Bayon of
Angkor Thom. Sandstone. Cambodia, reign of Jayavarman VII, ca. 1181-1218.
W. 34-1/2 in. 38.433

Padmapani. Copper. Java, Sailendra
Period, 8th-9th century. H. 6-1/8 in.
54.125

Head of Buddha. Black lava stone.
Java, from Borobudur, early 9th
century. H. 12 in. 42.1087

Vase: Pan-shan Type. Painted pottery. China, Kansu Province, Neolithic Period, 2500-1500 B.C. H. 14-1/4 in. 30.332

Ting: Tripod. Bronze. China, Shang Dynasty, 11th century B.C. H. 9-5/8 in. 62.281

Axe. Bronze. China, Shang Dynasty, 1523-1028 B.C. H. 8-5/16 in. 37.27

Fang-yu: Square Wine Container. Bronze. China, late Shang Dynasty, 12th-11th century B.C. H. 10-1/2 in. 63.103*

Ku: Beaker. Bronze. China, Shang Dynasty, 13th-12th century B.C. H. 10-9/16 in. 60.43

Mask. Marble. China, Shang Dynasty, ca. 1200 B.C. W. 5-1/4 in. 52.585

245

Elephant-feline Head. Jade, partly calcified. China, Shang Dynasty, ca. 1200 B.C. L. 1-5/8 in. 52.573

Tsun: Owl Wine Vessel. Bronze. China, early Western Chou Period, 1027-771 B.C. H. 8-1/4 in. 51.119

Tsun: Ceremonial Vessel. Bronze. China, early Chou Period, 1027-ca. 900 B.C. H. 11-5/8 in. 51.151

Li-ting: Hollow-legged Tripod. Bronze. China, reportedly from Hsi-an middle Western Chou Period, ca. 950-ca. 900 B.C. D. 10-7/8 in. 61.203*

Hu: Covered Vessel. Bronze. China, middle Chou Period, ca. 900-ca. 600 B.C. H. 18-1/8 in. 44.61

Staff Finial. Bronze. China, from Chin-Ts'un, Period of Warring States, ca. 481-221 B.C. H. 5-5/16 in. 30.730*

Po: Bell. Bronze. China, late Chou Period, early 5th century B.C. H. 16-1/4 in. 62.44

Cranes and Serpents. Lacquered wood. China, from Ch'ang-sha, Period of Warring States, 481-221 B.C. H. 52 in. 38.9*

Interlace Plaque. Honey-colored jade. China, from Ch'ang-sha, late Chou Period, ca. 600-211 B.C. W. 2-15/16 in. 52.584

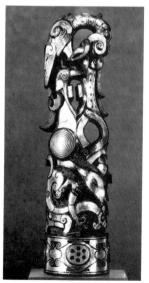

The Kill. Carved and painted shell. China, late Chou or early Han Dynasty, 3rd-2nd century B.C. W. 3-1/2 in. 57.139

Hill Jar. Lead-glazed pottery. China, Han Dynasty, 206 B.C.-A.D. 220. H. 10-1/2 in. 48.214

Tomb Relief. Stone. China, from Szuch'üan, Han Dynasty, 206 B.C.- A.D. 220. H. 47-1/4 in. 62.280

Vase with Cover. Green lead glaze over red clay body. China, Han Dynasty, 206 B.C.-A.D. 220. H. 18-1/2 in. 24.196

Vase. Porcelain with ash glaze. China, early Han Dynasty, 2nd century B.C. H. 18 in. 54.370

Top of a Hun-p'ing: Urn of the Soul.
Yueh ware. China, from Shao-hsing.
Six Dynasties, Wu Dynasty, 222-280,
or Western Chin Dynasty, 265-316.
D. 8-1/2 in. 60.76

Pole Top: Wild Ass. Cast bronze,
hollow. China, Ordos Region, Han
Dynasty, 206 B.C.-A.D. 220. H. 7 in.
62.46

*Two Reliefs from a Funerary Stove
Model.* Terra cotta. China, Han
Dynasty, 206 B.C.-A.D. 220.
W. 10-3/4 in. 25.134, 25.135

Tomb Tile (detail). Terra cotta. China, late Han Dynasty, 2nd-3rd century.
W. 41-1/2 in. 15.70

249

P'u-shou: Monster-headed Door-ring Holder. Gilt bronze. China, late Six Dynasties, 220-589. W. 7-7/8 in. 30.731

Maitreya and Attendants. Dated 500. Limestone. China, Northern Wei Period. H. 37-1/4 in. 59.130

Adoring Monk. Gilt bronze. China, Northern Wei Period, ca. 520-525. H. 5-7/8 in. 62.213

Mortuary Horse. Painted Pottery. China, Northern Wei Period, ca. 525. H. 8-3/4 in. 29.985

Head of Bodhisattva. Stone. China, from Lung-men, Northern Wei Period, ca. 510-520. H. 14-1/4 in. 15.77

Stele: Sakyamuni Trinity. Dated 537.
Limestone. China, Eastern Wei
Period. H. 30-1/2 in. 14.567

Squatting Caryatid Monster.
Limestone. China, from Northern
Hsiang-t'ang-shan, Northern Ch'i
Period, ca. 570. H. 29-1/2 in.
57.360

Stele: Maitreya, as the Future Buddha.
Marble. China, Northern Ch'i
Period, 550-577. H. 34 in. 17.320

Bodhisattva Kuan-yin. Sandstone
with polychrome. China, late
Northern Ch'i Period or early Sui
Dynasty, 575-600. H. 54-5/8 in.
62.162

Seated Sakyamuni Buddha. Limestone.
China, Sui Dynasty, 590-620
H. 20-1/4 in. 64.152

Guardian Lion. White marble. China,
Sui Dynasty or early T'ang Dynasty,
ca. 600. H. 31 in. 65.473

251

Candlestick. White porcellaneous ware, greenish-white glaze. China, Sui Dynasty, 581-618, or early T'ang Dynasty, 618-907. H. 11-3/4 in. 30.322

Horse. Pottery with polychrome glaze *(T'ang san-tsai).* China, T'ang Dynasty, 618-907. H. 30-1/4 in. 55.295

Jar. Pottery with polychrome glaze *(T'ang san-tsai).* China, T'ang Dynasty, 618-907. H. 5-1/8 in. 40.44

A Harpist. Pottery with traces of glaze. China, T'ang Dynasty, 618-907. H. 12-5/8 in. 31.450

Camel. Glazed pottery. China, T'ang Dynasty, 618-907. H. 31-1/2 in. 67.147

Bull. Painted pottery. China, T'ang Dynasty, 618-907. H. 6-3/16 in. 29.987

252

Jar. Cream-glaze pottery. China,
T'ang Dynasty, 618-907. H. 11 in.
30.323

Stem Cup. Gilded silver. China
T'ang Dynasty, 618-907. H. 3-1/2 in.
51.396

Jar. Porcelain, Hsing ware. China,
T'ang Dynasty, 618-907. H. 5 in.
57.29

Standing Kuan-yin. Limestone with
traces of polychrome. China, T'ang
Dynasty, dated 687, reportedly from
Pai-ma-ssu, Honan Province.
H. 67-1/4 in. 66.364

Kuan-yin. Marble. China, from Ling-yen-shan, Hopei, early T'ang Dynasty, 618-907. H. 70 in. 29.981

Eleven-headed Kuan-yin. Gray sandstone. China, T'ang Dynasty, 1st quarter 8th century. H. 51 in. 59.129*

Ewer in the Form of a Court Lady. Porcellaneous ware. North China, Liao Kingdom, 947-1125. H. 8-3/8 in. 53.248

Dancing Apsara. Dry lacquer. China, late T'ang Dynasty or early Five Dynasties, 9th-10th century. H. 15-3/4 in. 53.356

Textile. Silk, patterned weave. China, 8th century. H. 10-9/16 in. 54.109

Seated Amitabha Buddha. Gilt bronze.
China, Liao Kingdom, 10th century.
H. 9 in. 42.1082

Taoist Figure. Wood and ivory.
China, Southern Sung Dynasty,
1127-1279. H. 12-1/2 in. 64.368

Potala Kuan-yin. Wood (loquat).
China, Five Dynasties, 10th century.
H. 5-15/16 in. 65.556

Bodhisattva. Cypress. China, Chin
Dynasty, 13th century. H. 57-1/2 in.
63.581

Vase. Stoneware, Tz'u-chou ware.
China, Sung Dynasty or earlier,
960-1279. H. 12-5/8 in. 42.656

Jar. Stoneware, Tz'u-chou ware.
China, Sung Dynasty, 960-1279.
H. 13-3/4 in. 48.225

Meip'ing: Gallipot Vase. Stoneware,
Tz'u-chou ware. China, Northern
Sung Dynasty, 960-1127. H. 13-1/2 in.
40.52

Vase. Stoneware, Tz'u-chou ware,
"Chiao-ts'o" type. China, Northern
Sung Dynasty, 960-1127. H. 16-1/4 in.
48.226*

Lion. Porcelain, Yüeh ware. China,
Northern Sung Dynasty, 960-1127.
H. 7-1/8 in. 66.26

Teapot. Stoneware, Tz'u-chou ware.
China, Sung Dynasty, 960-1279.
H. 6-7/8 in. 48.219

Phoenix-headed Vase. Porcelain,
Ch'ing-pai ware. China, Northern
Sung Dynasty, 960-1127.
H. 15-3/8 in. 65.468*

Covered Box. White porcelain, Ting ware. China, Northern Sung Dynasty, 960-1127. D. 4-1/8 in. 57.32

Circular Washer. Porcelain, Ju ware. China, Northern Sung Dynasty, 960-1127. D. 5-1/16 in. 57.40

Covered Box with Carved Floral Design. Porcelain, northern celadon ware. China, Northern Sung Dynasty, 960-1127. D. 4-3/16 in. 62.41

Plate. Porcellaneous stoneware, Chun ware. China, Sung Dynasty, 960-1279 D. 7-1/8 in. 42.665

Teapot. Porcelain, Tung ware. China, Northern Sung Dynasty, 960-1127. H. 7-3/8 in. 48.220*

Flower Pot Stand. Porcellaneous stoneware, Chun ware. China, Sung Dynasty, 960-1279. D. 9-1/4 in. 57.33

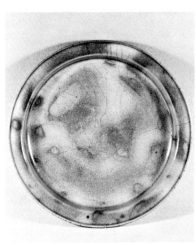

Ting: Tripod. Celadon, Lung-ch'üan ware. China, Southern Sung Dynasty, 1127-1279. D. 5-1/2 in. 54.790

Althea Bowl. Kuan ware. China, Southern Sung Dynasty, 1127-1279. D. 6-7/8 in. 57.66

Ch'a-tou: Vase in Grain Measure Shape. Lung-ch'üan ware. China, Southern Sung Dynasty, 1127-1279. H. 3-9/16 in. 57.73

Lu: Incense Burner. Porcellaneous stoneware, Kuan ware. China, Southern Sung Dynasty, 1127-1279. W. 6-1/8 in. 57.63*

Washer Basin. From Phoenix Hill Kiln, Hangchou, Kuan ware. China, Southern Sung Dynasty, 1127-1279 D. 9-1/2 in. 57.48

258

Buddhist Monastery by Stream and Mountains. Hanging scroll, ink on silk. Attributed to Chü-jan, Chinese, active ca. 960-980, Northern Sung Dynasty. H. 73 in. 59.348*

Barbarian Royalty Worshiping Buddha. Handscroll, ink and color on silk. Traditionally attributed to Chao Kuang-fu, Chinese, active 960-975. Northern Sung Dynasty. W. 40-3/4 in. 57.358

Ch'i-shan wu-chin: Streams and Mountains Without End. (detail). Handscroll, ink on silk. China, Northern Sung Dynasty, early 12th century. W. 83-7/8 in. 53.126*

Cloudy Mountains (detail). Dated 1130. Handscroll, ink and slight color on silk. Mi Yu-jen, Chinese, Sung Dynasty. W. 76-1/2 in. 33.220*

Cottages in a Misty Grove in Autumn.
Dated 1117. Album leaf, ink and color
on silk. Li An-chung, Chinese,
Northern Sung Dynasty. H. 10-2/3 in.
63.588

Bamboo and Ducks by a Rushing Stream.
Hanging scroll, ink and light color
on silk. Ma Yuan, Chinese, active
ca. 1190-ca. 1224, Southern Sung
Dynasty, H. 24 in. 67.145

*Birds in a Grove in a Mountainous
Landscape in Winter.* Hanging scroll,
ink and slight color on silk. Kao
Tao(?), Chinese, Sung Dynasty,
12th century. H. 68-7/8 in. 66.115

The Knick-Knack Peddler. Dated 1201. Album leaf, ink
and slight color on silk. Li Sung, Chinese, Southern Sung
Dynasty. H. 9-1/2 in. 63.582*

Scholar Reclining and Watching Rising Clouds. Dated 1256.
Fan painting, ink and slight color on silk. Ma Lin,
Chinese, Southern Sung Dynasty. H. 9-15/16 in. 61.421

Tiger. Hanging scroll, ink on silk. Attributed to Mu-ch'i, Chinese, active 2nd half 13th century, Southern Sung Dynasty. H. 48-3/4 in. 58.428

Plate with Biscuit Dragon. Porcelain with celadon glaze. China, Yüan Dynasty, 14th century. D. 17 in. 61.92

The Bodhisattva P'u-hsien: Samantabhadra. Hanging scroll, color and ink on silk. China, Southern Sung Dynasty, 1127-1279. H. 45-3/16 in. 62.161

Jar with Lion-head Handles. Porcelain with blue underglaze decoration. China, Yüan Dynasty, 14th century. H. 15-1/2 in. 62.154

Jar. Tz'u-chou ware. China, Yüan Dynasty, 1279-1368. H. 11 in. 48.215

Bowl with Taoist Designs. White jade (nephrite). China, Yüan Dynasty, late 13th to early 14th century. W. 6-1/4 in. 52.510

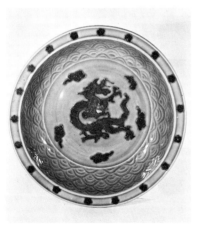

The Lantern Night Excursion of Chung K'uei (detail). Handscroll, ink on silk. Yen Hui, Chinese, Yüan Dynasty, 1279-1368. W. 94-5/8 in. 61.206

Sakyamuni as an Ascetic. Gilt bronze. China, Yüan Dynasty, early 14th century. H. 17-3/8 in. 66.116

Chiu-ko-t'u: The Nine Songs (detail). Handscroll, ink on paper. Chang Wu, Chinese, active 1335-1365, Yüan Dynasty. W. 14 ft. 4-1/2 in. 59.138

The Second Coming of the Fifth Patriarch. Section of a handscroll mounted as a hanging scroll, ink on paper. Yin-t'o-lo (Indara), Chinese, active ca. mid-14th century, Yüan Dynasty. W. 17-9/16 in. 67.211

Bodhidharma Crossing the Yangtze on a Reed. Hanging scroll, ink on paper. China, Yüan Dynasty, 1279-1368. H. 35-1/8 in. 64.44

Three Horses and Four Grooms (detail). Handscroll, ink and color on silk. Jen Jen-fa, Chinese, 1254-1327, early Yüan Dynasty. W. 53-7/8 in. 60.181

Ink Flowers (detail). Dated 1361. Handscroll, ink on paper. Chao Chung, Chinese, active ca. 2nd half 14th century, Yüan Dynasty. W. 60-5/16 in. 67.36

Bamboos, Rocks, and Lonely Orchids (detail), Handscroll, ink on paper. Chao Meng-fu, Chinese, 1254-1322, Yüan Dynasty. W. 56-3/4 in. 63.515*

Poetic Feeling in a Thatched Pavilion (detail). Dated 1347. Handscroll, ink on paper. Wu Chen, Chinese, Yüan Dynasty. W. 39-1/8 in. 63.259

Leisure Enough to Spare. Dated 1360. Handscroll, ink on paper. Yao T'ing-mei, Chinese, Yüan Dynasty. W. 33-1/16 in. 54.791

263

Chrysanthemums and Cabbage (detail). Dated 1490. Handscroll, ink and slight color on paper. T'ao Cheng, Chinese, Ming Dynasty. W. 40 in. 60.40

The Poet Lin P'u Wandering in the Moonlight. Hanging scroll, ink and slight color on paper. Tu Chin, Chinese, active ca. 1465-1487, Ming Dynasty. H. 61-5/8 in. 54.582

Wu-she-shan: The Mountain of the Five Cataracts. Hanging scroll, ink on silk. Ch'en Hung-shou, Chinese, 1598-1652, Ming Dynasty. H. 46-9/16 in. 66.366

A Distant View of Tiger Hill, from *Twelve Views of Tiger Hill, Suchou.* Album leaf, ink on paper. Shen Chou, Chinese, 1427-1509, Ming Dynasty. W. 15-13/16 in. 64.371*

Old Pine Tree. Handscroll, ink on paper. Wen Cheng-ming, Chinese
1470-1559, Ming Dynasty. W. 56 in. 64.43

Beggars and Street Characters (detail). Dated 1516.
Handscroll, ink and color on paper. Chou Ch'en, Chinese,
Ming Dynasty. W. 96-1/4 in. 64.94

*Chao Meng-fu Writing the Heart Sutra in Exchange for
Tea* (detail). Dated 1543. Color on paper. Ch'iu Ying,
Chinese, Ming Dynasty. W. 30-5/8 in. 63.102

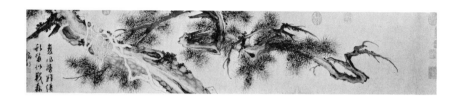

Mountains on a Clear Autumn Day. Tribute from the Korean king to the throne of Ming Emperor Sheng-tsung. Handscroll, ink on paper. Tung Ch'i-ch'ang, Chinese, 1555-1636, Ming Dynasty. W. 53-7/8 in. 59.46

Greeting the Spring (detail). Dated 1600. Handscroll, color and ink on paper. Wu Pin, Chinese, Ming Dynasty. W. 96-1/2 in. 59.45

Lady Hsüan-wen-chün Giving Instructions on the Classics. Dated 1638. Hanging scroll, color on silk. Ch'en Hung-shou, Chinese, Ming Dynasty. H. 68-3/8 in. 61.89

Chüeh: Libation Cup. Imperial white porcelain. China, Ming Dynasty, reign of Yung-lo, 1403-1424. H. 5-7/8 in. 57.59

Pa-pei: Stem Cup. Porcelain, blue underglaze, red enamel overglaze. China, Ming Dynasty, mark and reign of Hsüan-te, 1426-1435. H. 3-1/2 in. 57.60

Dish. Porcelain with underglaze in Mohammedan blue. China, Ming Dynasty, reign of Hsüan-te, 1426-1435. D. 17 in. 53.127*

Wine Cup. Porcelain with blue underglaze and overglaze in red and green enamels, Tou Tsai ware. China, Ming Dynasty, mark and reign of Ch'eng-hua, 1465-1487. H. 1-7/8 in. 57.61*

Bowl with Land of Taoist Immortals Scene. Porcelain with blue underglaze decoration. China, Ming Dynasty, mark and reign of Hsüan-te, 1426-1435. D. 7-3/4 in. 62.260

Dice Bowl with Decoration of the "Three Friends." Porcelain with blue underglaze decoration. China, Ming Dynasty, mark and reign of Hsüan-te, 1426-1435. D. 11-7/8 in. 53.631

Bowl. Porcelain with blue underglaze decoration. China, Ming Dynasty, mark and reign of Ch'eng-hua, 1465-1487. D. 5-11/16 in. 67.64

Kuan-yin of the South Sea. White porcelain, Te-hua ware. China, Ming Dynasty, 1368-1644. H. 17-3/4 in. 50.579

Vase. Porcelain, "yellow family." China, Ming Dynasty, 1368-1644. H. 17 in. 42.718

Vase, "Fa-hua" type. Porcelain. China, Shansi Province, Ming Dynasty, late 15th century. H. 14-3/4 in. 42.716

Covered Jar. Porcelain, blue underglaze, overglaze in red, green, and yellow enamels. China, Ming Dynasty, mark and reign of Wan-li, 1573-1619. H. 4 in. 57.62

Reclining Water Buffalo. Jade. China, early Ming Dynasty, 1368-1644. L. 8-1/4 in. 60.282

Hoop-backed Armchair, "Lohan Type,"
Huang-hua-li, Burmese or East
Indian rosewood. China, late Ming
Dynasty, 17th century. H. 33-5/8 in.
55.40

Fragment of a Panel. Tapestry weave
(k'o-ssu), silk and gold. China,
Ming Dynasty, 1368-1644. H. 78 in.
16.1334

Fish and Rocks (detail). Handscroll,
ink on paper. Chu Ta, Chinese, 1624-
ca. 1705, Ch'ing Dynasty. W. 62 in.
53.247

Pure Tones of the Hills and Waters (detail). Dated 1664.
Handscroll, ink and color on paper. Hsiao Yun-ts'ung,
Chinese, Ch'ing Dynasty. W. 25 ft. 7-3/4 in. 54.262

Strolling Companions in the Autumn Mountains. Double
album leaf mounted as a handscroll, ink and color on
paper. K'un-ts'an, Chinese, active 2nd half 17th
century. Ch'ing Dynasty. W. 25-3/8 in. 66.367

Reminiscences of Ch'in-Huai River.
Album leaf, ink and color on paper.
Shih-t'ao (Tao-chi), Chinese, 1641-
ca. 1720, Ch'ing Dynasty.
H. 10-1/16 in. 66.31*

Pine Wind from Myriad Valleys.
Hanging scroll, ink and color on
paper. Wu Li, Chinese, 1632-1718,
Ch'ing Dynasty. H. 43-1/8 in. 54.584

*Tall Bamboos and Distant Mountains
After Wang Meng.* Dated 1694.
Hanging scroll, ink on paper.
Wang Hui, Chinese, Ch'ing Dynasty.
H. 31-1/4 in. 53.629

Conversation in Autumn. Dated 1732.
Hanging scroll, ink and color on
paper. Hua Yen, Chinese, Ch'ing
Dynasty. H. 45-3/8 in. 54.263*

Landscape After Ni Tsan. Dated 1707.
Hanging scroll, ink and color on
paper. Wang Yuan-ch'i, Chinese,
Ch'ing Dynasty. H. 31-5/8 in. 54.583

*Drunken Chung K'uei Supported by
Ghosts.* Hanging scroll, ink and
color on paper. Lo P'ing, Chinese,
1733-1799, Ch'ing Dynasty.
H. 38-1/8 in. 59.185

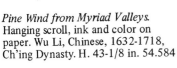

270

Bottle-shaped Vase. Lang ware, "ox-blood" glaze. China, Ch'ing Dynasty, reign of K'ang-hsi, 1662-1722. H. 15 in. 44.201

Vase. Porcelain, "peach-bloom" glaze. China, Ch'ing Dynasty, mark and reign of K'ang-hsi, 1662-1722. H. 8-5/16 in. 42.669

Baluster Vase. Porcelain, "black family." China, Ch'ing Dynasty, reign of K'ang-hsi, 1662-1722. H. 17-3/8 in. 42.696

Vase. Porcelain, "soft paste," blue underglaze. China, Ch'ing Dynasty, mark and reign of Yung-cheng, 1723-1735. H. 11-1/4 in. 42.728

Vase. Porcelain, "green family."
China, Ch'ing Dynasty, reign of
K'ang-hsi, 1662-1722. H. 10-3/4 in.
42.685

Vase, Ku-yüeh-hsüan Type. Porcelain
with decoration in colored *fa-lang*
enamels. China, Ch'ing Dynasty,
mark and reign of Ch'ien-lung,
1736-1795. H. 6-1/16 in. 63.514

Vase, Ku-yüeh-hsüan Type. Porcelain
"rouge de fer" handles, black and
colored enamels. China, Ch'ing
Dynasty, reign of Ch'ien-lung,
1736-1795. H. 10-3/4 in. 42.712

Koro with T'ao-t'ieh Masks. Green
jade. China, Ch'ing Dynasty, Ch'ien-
lung Period, 1736-1795. H. 6 in.
42.620

Vase. Porcelain. Korea, Koryu Period, 12th or 13th century. H. 10 in. 44.164

Bottle Vase with Fish Design. Punch'ong stoneware. Korea, Yi Dynasty, 15th century. H. 12 in. 62.153

Haniwa Figure. Terra cotta. Japan, Kofun Period, ca. 6th century. H. 23 in. 62.39

Dotaku: Bell. Bronze. Japan, late Yayoi Period, 100-300. H. 38-1/2 in. 16.1102

Urn. Terra cotta. Japan, middle Jomon Period, ca. 1000 B.C. H. 15-1/2 in. 60.196

Heavenly Musician. From Horyu-ji
Nara. Camphor wood with polychrome.
Japan, Hakuho Period, 645-710.
H. 21-1/8 in. 54.792

Kannon: Avalokiteshvara. Gilt
bronze. Japan, Hakuho Period,
645-710. H. 13 in. 50.392

*Hanka-shiyui-zo: Bodhisattva in
Meditation.* Bronze. Japan, Suiko
Period, 7th century. H. 18 in. 50.86

Woman from an Audience Scene.
Probably from Horyu-ji, Nara. Gray
unbaked clay. Japan, Hakuho Period,
645-710. H. 7-1/2 in. 50.393

Suikoju: Gigaku Mask. Paulownia
wood, lacquered and painted. Japan,
Tempyo Period, 710-794. H. 11 in.
49.158

Hand of Buddha. Wood. Japan, late Nara or early Jogan Period, late 8th-early 9th century. H. 15-3/4 in. 56.126

Bosatsu, Gyodo Mask. Lacquered wood with paint. Japan, Fujiwara Period, late 12th century. H. 8-5/8 in. 50.581

Nikko, the Sun Bodhisattva. Carved from one block of Japanese yew. Japan, Konin Period, ca. 800. H. 18-3/8 in. 61.48

Amida's Paradise. Lacquer, fragment mounted as a box cover. Japan, late Heian Period, ca. 1200. W. 5-3/16 in. 61.91

Godai-Kokuzo: Five Bodhisattvas of the Mandala of the Void. Gilded wood. Japan, Fujiwara Period, 897-1185. H. (central figure) 7-5/16 in. 64.45-64.49

Box with Chrysanthemum Design. Lacquer. Japan, Kamakura Period, 1185-1333. W. 10-3/4 in. 63.513

Kannon. Lacquered wood with *kirikane* decoration. Japan, Kamakura Period, 13th century. H. 30 in. 52.90

Shinto Deity: Izu-san Gongen. Wood. Japan, Kamakura Period, 12th-13th century. H. 39-3/8 in. 54.373

Amida, Buddha of the Western Paradise. Dated 1269. Wood with cut gold leaf, polychrome. Koshun and assistants, Japanese, Kamakura Period. H. 37-1/4 in. 60.197

Kara-shishi ("China Lion"). Wood. Japan, Kamakura Period. H. 19-1/2 in. 24.352

276

Gohimitsu Bosatsu: The "Secret Five" Bodhisattva. Hanging scroll, color, gold, and silver on three joined pieces of silk. Japan, Kamakura Period, late 12th century. H. 31-1/16 in. 61.423*

White-robed Kannon from Kozan-ji. Hanging scroll, ink on paper. Japan, Kamakura Period, ca. 1200. H. 36 in. 51.540

Nika Byakudo: The White Path to the Western Paradise Across Two Rivers. Hanging scroll, ink and color on silk. Japan, Kamakura Period, 13th-14th century. H. 48-5/8 in. 55.44

One of the "Ten Fast Bulls." Hanging scroll, ink and slight color on paper, from a handscroll. Japan, Kamakura Period, mid-13th century. W. 12-5/8 in. 52.286

Kumano Mandala: The Three Sacred Shrines. Hanging scroll, color on silk. Japan, Kamakura Period, ca. 1300. H. 52-3/4 in. 53.16

277

The Poet Taira-No-Kanemori. Section of a handscroll, black, white, and slight color on paper. Japan, Kamakura Period, 1185-1333. W. 18-3/8 in. 51.397

Choyo: Priest Sewing Under the Morning Sun. Hanging scroll, ink on paper. Ca. 1350 or slightly earlier. Kao, Japanese, Nambochuko Period. H. 32-15/16 in. 62.163

Yuzu Nembutsu Engi: Efficacy of Repeated Invocations to the Amida Buddha (detail). Handscroll, ink, color, and gold on paper. Japan, Kamakura Period, 14th century. W. 42 ft. 2-1/2 in. 56.87

Fukutomi Zoshi (detail). Handscroll, ink and color on paper. Japan, Kamakura Period, 14th century. W. 33 ft. 8-3/4 in. 53.358

278

Haboku Landscape. Hanging scroll, ink on paper. Sesshu, Japanese, 1420-1506, Muromachi Period. H. 28-5/16 in. 55.43

Winter and Spring Landscape. Six-fold screen, ink and slight color on paper. Shubun, Abbot of Shokoku-ji, Kyoto, Japanese, ca. 1390-1464, Muromachi Period. W. 12 ft. 58.476*

Birds and Flowers in a Winter and Spring Landscape. One of a pair of six-fold screens, ink and color on paper. Attributed to Sesshu, Japanese, 1420-1506, Muromachi Period. W. 12 ft. 3 in. 61.204

Eight Scenes of Hsiao-Hsiang. Hanging scroll, ink on paper. Ca. 1509. So-ami, Japanese, Muromachi Period. H. 50-5/8 in. 63.262*

Horses and Grooms (detail). One of a pair of six-fold screens, color and ink on paper. Japan, Muromachi Period, 1392-1573. W. 12 ft. 1 in. 34.374

Kasuga Mandala. Hanging scroll, ink on silk. Japan, Muromachi Period, 1392-1573. H. 47 in. 17.93

Dragon and Tiger. Pair of six-fold screens, ink on paper. Sesson, Japanese, born 1504-active until 1589, Muromachi Period. W. 12 ft. 59.136, 59.137*

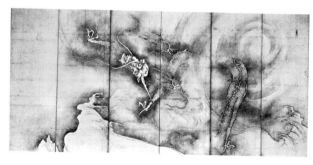

Namban Byobu: "Southern Barbarians" Scenes. One of a pair of six-fold screens. Color on paper. 1610-1614. Japan, Momoyama or early Edo Period. W. 11 ft. 6-1/4 in. 60.193

Table. Wood, lacquer, gold, and silver. Japan, Muromachi Period, 15th century. W. 23 in. 58.429

Cosmetic Box. Lacquer, Japan, Momoyama Period, 1573-1615. W. 13-1/8 in. 66.25

Bowl with Cross. Glazed stoneware, Hagi ware. Japan, Momoyama Period, ca. 1600. H. 9-1/8 in. 62.211

Dish with Design of Three Wild Geese in Flight. Pottery, Nezumi Shino ware. Japan, Momoyama Period, ca. 1600. D. 6-1/2 in. 59.35

Ewer. Pottery, Oribe ware. Japan, Momoyama Period, 1573-1615. H. 8-1/4 in. 58.336

Dish with Design of Valerian and Rocks in a Garden. Pottery, Nezumi Shino ware. Japan, Momoyama Period, ca. 1610. Reportedly from the Inkyo Nishi Kiln at Kujiri. W 9-3/16 in. 66.24

282

Scene from the Ise Monogatari: The Beach at Sumiyoshi. Album leaf, color and gold on paper. Nonomura Sotatsu, Japanese, Edo Period, early 17th century. H. 9-5/8 in. 51.398

Sano-no-Watari: Crossing at Sano. Screen, ink on gold-ground paper. Nonomura Sotatsu, Japanese, Edo Period, early 17th century. H. 51 in. 49.554

Chrysanthemums by a Stream. One of a pair of six-fold screens, color and gold leaf on paper. Ogata Korin, Japanese, 1658-1716, Edo Period. W. 12 ft. 4 in. 58.207

Utsunoyama: The Pass Through the Mountains. Six-fold screen, color on gold-ground paper. Fukaye Roshu, Japanese, 1699-1757, Edo Period. W. 8 ft. 11 in. 54.127*

*Calligraphy by Koetsu of Waka, Poems from "Shin-kokinshu"
Written over Designs by Sotatsu* (detail). Handscroll,
ink, gold, silver, and color on paper. Japan, Edo Period,
early 17th century. W. 11 ft. 4-1/2 in. 66.118

Irises. One of a pair of six-fold screens, ink and color
on gold-ground paper. Watanabe Shiko, Japanese, 1683-1755,
Edo Period. W. 11 ft. 10 in. 54.604

Thirty-six Poets. Two-fold screen, color on paper.
Attributed to Tatebayashi Kagei, Japanese, Edo Period,
1st half 18th century. W. 73-1/2 in. 60.183

Paulownias and Chrysanthemums. Two-fold screen, color
and gold on paper. Sakai Hoitsu, Japanese, 1779-1828,
Edo Period. W. 62-3/8 in. 64.386

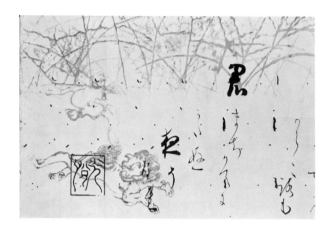

284

*Portrait of the Chinese Priest
Dokuritsu.* Dated 1671. Hanging scroll.
Kita Genki, Japanese, Edo Period.
H. 43-7/8 in. 65.31

Bamboo in Fine Weather After Rain. Two-fold screen, ink
on paper. Ike-no-Taiga, Japanese, 1723-1776, late Edo
Period. W. 71-3/4 in. 58.337

Forbidden to the Vulgar. Hanging
scroll, ink on paper. Uragami Gyokudo,
Japanese, 1745-1820, Edo Period.
H. 53 in. 64.367

The Actor Sanjo Kantaro. Color on
paper. Ca. 1714. Kaigetsudo Ando,
Japanese, Edo Period. H. 41-5/8 in.
61.41

Flowers of Four Seasons. One of a pair of six-fold
screens, ink and color on paper. Kitagawa Sosetsu,
Japanese, mid-17th century, Edo Period. W. 10 ft.
10-3/8 in. 68.193

Tzuzuri Bako: Writing Box. Lacquer. Japan, Edo Period, ca. 1800. W. 8-1/8 in. 63.260

Covered Bowl with Chrysanthemums and Chidori. Porcelain, Kakiemon ware, decorated in colored enamels. Japan, Edo Period, early 18th century. D. 8-1/4 in. 61.42

Standing Figure of a Beauty. Porcelain, Kakiemon-type ware. Japan, Edo Period, late 17th century H. 14-15/16 in. 64.366*

Plate with Bird and Flower. Porcelain, Kutani ware. Japan, Edo Period, 17th century. D. 11-3/4 in. 60.174

Dish with Design of Plovers over Waves. Pottery. Ca. 1700. Design by Ogata Korin, 1658-1716, dish by Ogata Kenzan, 1663-1743, Japanese Edo Period. W. 8-5/8 in. 66.365

Bowl (one of a pair). Porcelain. Kakiemon ware. Japan, Edo Period, late 17th century. D. 14 in. 64.364

Notes

Notes

Notes

Pre-Columbian Art

290

Jade Figurine. Mexico, Gulf Coast, Olmec, before 300. H. 4-5/16 in. 41.390*

Stone Axe. Mexico, Gulf Coast, Olmec, before 300. H. 12-5/8 in. 54.856

Seated Figure. Stone. Mexico, Gulf Coast, Olmec, before 300. H. 10-1/4 in. 51.179

Stone Head. Mexico, Olmec style, 1st-5th century. H. 6-1/2 in. 53.369

Jade Mask. Mexico, Gulf Coast, Olmec, before 300. H. 5-3/8 in. 67.154

Jade Head. Mexico, Western Mexico(?) Olmec style, 1st-5th century. H. 2-7/8 in. 61.31

291

Recumbent Anthropomorphic Figure. Stone. Mexico, Gulf Coast, 3rd-5th century(?). L. 16-9/16 in. 48.355

Terra-cotta Head. Mexico, Gulf Coast, Totonac or Tajin, 5th-9th century. H. 11-1/16 in. 40.11*

Painted Terra-cotta Head. Mexico, Gulf Coast, Totonac or Tajin, 5th-9th century. H. 6-3/4 in. 47.26

Seated Figure. Terra cotta. Mexico, Oaxaca, Monte Alban II (Zapotec), before Christ(?). H. 12-11/16 in. 54.857*

Dog. Earthenware. Mexico, Colima, 6th-7th century(?). H. 15-5/8 in. 64.37

292

Gold Shell with Bells. Mexico, Oaxaca, Mixtec, after 1000. H. 3 in. 52.86

Monkey. Stone. Mexico, Tacubaya, Aztec, 15th century. H. 9-5/8 in. 59.125

Seated Figure of Tlaloc, the Rain God. Serpentine. Mexico, Aztec. H. 11-1/4 in. 66.361

Xochipilli, God of Flowers, Dance, and Games. Stone. Mexico, Aztec, 15th century. H. 10-7/8 in. 49.555

Mask. Turquoise mosaic and terra cotta. Mexico(?), ca. 1220. H. 5-7/16 in. 67.141

Stone Head. Honduras, Copan, Maya, 7th-8th century. H. 20-3/4 in. 53.154

Seated Figure. Incised shell. Guatemala, Maya, 3rd-5th century. H. 6-1/2 in. 65.550*

Incense Burner. Terra cotta. Mexico, Palenque Region, 7th-8th century. H. 41 in. 65.248*

Woman in Ceremonial Robes. Limestone relief. Mexico or Guatemala, Usumacinta Region, Maya, ca. 795. H. 23-3/4 in. 62.32*

Vase. Earthenware with painted decoration. Guatemala, Kixpec, Maya, 8th-10th century. H. 6-1/2 in. 54.391

Relief: Part of a Stele. Limestone. Maya, 7th-8th century. H. 9 ft. 67.29

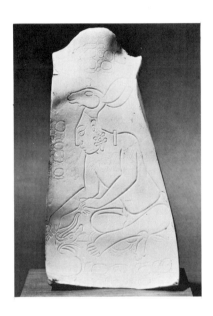

Figure of a Warrior. Terra cotta. Mexico, Yucatan, Island of Guaymil, Maya, 9th-10th century. H. 10-1/4 in. 63.93

Eccentric Flint in Human Shape. Stone. Guatemala, Quirigua, Maya, 6th-8th century. H. 13-5/8 in. 50.161*

Left: *Jade Head.* Honduras, Copan, Maya, 7th-8th century. H. 3 in. 47.176
Center: *Jadeite Pendant.* Mexico or Central America, Maya, 6th-8th century. H. 2-1/2 in. 52.119
Right: *Plaque.* Crystalline green stone. Mexico or Central America, Maya, 7th-9th century. H. 1-7/8 in. 50.153

Jaguar Macehead. Stone. Costa Rica, Nicoya, Chorotegan, 8th-9th century. H. 3-7/16 in. 49.469

Gold Plaque. Panama, Coclé, 14th-15th century. H. 9-7/8 in. 52.459*

295

Anthropomorphic Seated Figure.
Gold. Colombia, Quimbaya, 14th-15th
century. H. 2-7/8 in. 39.509*

Bird (Head of a Staff?). Gold.
Colombia, Quimbaya, 14th-15th century.
H. 2-15/16 in. 54.594

Double Puma Staff Head. Gold.
Colombia, Quimbaya, 14th-15th
century. H. 3-1/4 in. 44.319

Gold Pin. Colombia, Quimbaya,
14th-15th century. H. 8-15/16 in.
47.30

Stirrup Jar. Earthenware. Peru,
Chavin, 1st millennium B.C.
H. 8-15/16 in. 68.192

Gold Spoon. Peru, North Coast,
Chavin, 1st millennium B.C.
L. 6-7/8 in. 58.177*

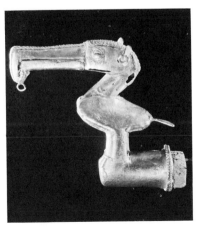

Gold Plaque. Peru, North Coast,
Chavin, 1st millennium B.C.
H. 8-9/16 in. 46.117

Finial in the Form of a Monkey. Gold.
Peru, North Coast, Mochica,
1st-5th century. H. 14-1/2 in. 49.197

Bowl with Incised Decoration. Stone.
Peru, North Coast, Chavin, 1st
millennium B.C. H. 2-9/16 in. 55.167

Border of a Mantle. Painted cotton. Peru, South Coast, Early Period.
Over-all: W. 8 ft. 4 in. Detail: W. 27 in. 40.530*

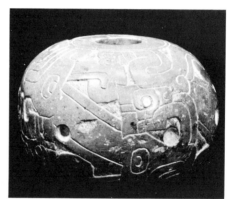

Poncho. Needle *réseau,* wool. Peru, South Coast, Paracas, Early Period. H. 37 in. 40.514

Poncho. Embroidery, wool. Peru, South Coast, Paracas, Early Period. H. 58 in. 46.227

Part of a Mantle. Embroidery, wool. Peru, South Coast, Paracas, Early Period. Over-all: W. 54-3/4 in. Detail: H. 18-1/2 in. 40.528

Mosaic Relief. Peru, North(?) Coast, Tiahuanaco, 9th-10th century. H. 2-9/16 in. 44.291

Jar. Earthenware with painted decoration. Peru, South Coast, Tiahuanaco, 10th-12th century. H. 14-7/16 in. 55.173

Textile. Tapestry weave, wool and cotton. Peru, South Coast, Tiahuanaco Culture, Middle Period. H. 15-1/2 in. 57.495

Poncho. Tapestry weave, wool and cotton. Peru, South Coast, Tiahuanaco Culture, Middle Period. H. 43 in. 56.84

Square Hat. Pile knot technique, wool. Peru, South Coast, Middle Period. H. 5-5/8 in. 45.378

Front of a Litter. Painted wood. Peru, North Coast, Chimu, 12th-13th century. H. 23-3/4 in. 52.233*

Poncho. Tapestry weave, wool and cotton. Peru, South Coast, Inca Culture, 1400-1532. H. 33-1/2 in. 57.136

Half Poncho. Tapestry weave, wool and cotton. Peru, Inca Period, 16th century. H. 37-1/2 in. 51.393

Notes

Art of Primitive Peoples

302

Mule's Head from a Headpiece. Wood and metal. Africa, Republic of Mali, Bambara Tribe. H. 16 in. 35.307

Woman and Child (Maternity Group). Wood. Africa, Ivory Coast, Korhogo District, Senufo Tribe. H. 25 in. 61.198

Dance Mask (Satimbe?). Wood. Africa, Republic of Mali, Sanga District, Dogon Tribe. H. 43-3/4 in. 60.169

Miniature Mask. Cast gold. Africa, Ivory Coast, Baule Tribe. H. 2-15/16 in. 54.602

Snake. Painted wood. Africa, Guinea, Baga Tribe. Landuman Sub-tribe. H. 58-1/4 in. 60.37

Warrior-attendant Plaque. Bronze. Africa, Nigeria, Benin, 17th century. H. 19-7/16 in. 53.425

303

Altar Portrait of a Deceased Oba.
Bronze. Africa, Nigeria, Benin,
17th century. H. 11-3/4 in. 38.6

Dance Mask. Painted wood. Africa,
Republic of the Congo, Kasai Province,
Bushongo Tribe (Bakuba). H. 17 in.
35.304*

Helmet Mask. Wood. Africa, Cameroon
Grasslands. H. 22-1/2 in. 67.151

Pair of Lions. Wood. Africa, Dahomey. H. 14-1/8 in. 65.323-65.324

War Shield. Painted wood. Melanesia, Dutch New Guinea, Asmat. H. 69-1/4 in. 63.554

Kamanggabi Figure. Painted wood with cowrie-shell. Melanesia, New Guinea, Central Sepik River District, Arambak. H. 82-1/2 in. 63.553

Canoe Prow. Wood. Southeast New Guinea, Massim Area. Trobriand Islands, 19th century. H. 23-1/8 in. 66.130

Lintel. Wood. Polynesia, New Zealand, Maori. H. 13-3/4 in. 62.350

Ceremonial Adze. Wood, stone, fiber. Central Polynesia, Hervey Islands. L. 49 in. 40.1078

Staff: U'u (detail). Stained ironwood. Polynesia, Marquesas Islands. Over-all: H. 58-3/8 in. 63.255

Yoke. Wood. Polynesia, Easter Island. W. 27-1/2 in. 61.406

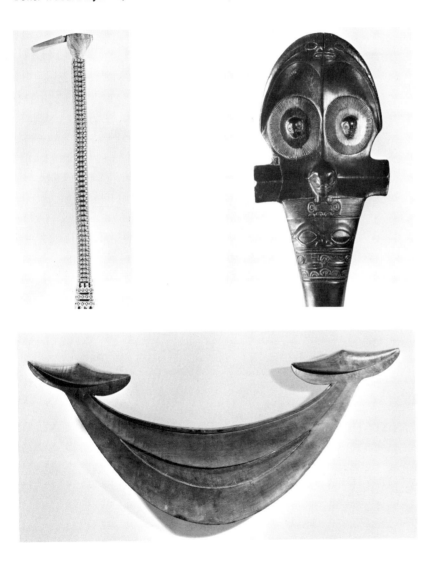

Notes